D1541104

First-Year Baby Care

An Illustrated Step-by-Step Guide For
New Parents

Edited by Paula Kelly, M.D.

Meadowbrook Press

18318 Minnetonka Boulevard
Deephaven, Minnesota 55391
Phone: (612) 473-5400

First printing July 1983

Printed in the United States of America

Library of Congress Cataloging in Publication Data

Main entry under title

First-year baby care.
   Includes index.
   1. Infants—Care and hygiene—Handbooks, manuals, etc. I. Kelly, Paula, 1949-
RJ61.F47   1983   649'.122   83-8361
ISBN 0-915658-05-4
ISBN 0-915658-03-8 (pbk.)

ISBN 0-915658-05-4 (hardcover)
ISBN 0-915658-03-8 (paperback)

Medical Editor: Paula Kelly, M.D.
Managing Editor: Thomas Grady
Writing/Research: Brigitte Frase, Mary Grady, Steve Grooms, Sharon Harrington, Mary Francois Rockcastle
Production Editor: Donna Ahrens
Production Manager: John Ware
Cover Design: Chuck Sathers
Text Design: John Ware
Interior Photographs: Michael Kehoe
Cover and Newborn Photographs: Creative Resource Center
Illustrations: Douglas Oudekerk

Special thanks to Melissa Avery, C.N.M., M.S.N.; Pamela Barnard; Mavis Brehm, R.N., B.S.N.; Mitch Einzig, M.D.; Kristine Ellis; Robert and Lindsay Collins; Jackson and John Gehan; Michael Grady; Alvin Handelman; Robin, Gregory, and Jasmaine Harris; Gail and Kevin Ketter; Bonnie Kinn; Pat, John, and Kevin Sevlie; Kate and Lily Shank; Sue and Diane Sherek; Peg and Meghan Short; Nancy and Nicholas Wood; and Sue and Sara Veazie.

Acknowledgements: to the Childbirth Education Association of Seattle, for permission to reprint the material on baby exercises, p. 85. Some of the material in the medical care section first appeared, in slightly different form, in **The Parents' Guide to Baby and Child Medical Care**, ed. by Terril H. Hart, M.D. (Meadowbrook, 1982).

10 9 8 7 6 5 4 3 2

TABLE OF CONTENTS

INTRODUCTION

Becoming a new parent is one of the most thrilling experiences you will ever have. You'll also be challenged in new ways, and you'll need to accept lots of new responsibilities. *First-Year Baby Care* has been written to help you during the time you'll need it most—your baby's first year. It's meant to give you confidence in your own abilities as a parent.

New babies grow and change very quickly during their first year. Just when you think you've understood one stage, your child will move into another. Every child and every family is unique, of course, but as both a pediatrician and a mother, I've learned that new parents often raise the same kinds of questions. They range from simple matters, like how to bathe your baby or child-proof your home, to more complicated ones about medical care and child development.

We've designed this book to answer the questions you have on how to care for your baby. It has been prepared by a team of writers and editors who are parents themselves and who understand the everyday concerns that new parents have. It is being published at a time when many new mothers are spending less time in the hospital after their children are born, giving them less opportunity to become familiar with many aspects of new baby care. The book is also important to parents who adopt children and don't have access to newborn classes.

We also realize that, as a new parent, you won't have time to read a lengthy text or hunt for information when you need it quickly. We have presented the information you need in an easily accessible and understandable form, and we've supplied photographs and illustrations where they are most useful.

Your baby's first year will challenge you and give you many moments of great joy. I hope this book helps you respond to the challenge and realize the joy.

Paula Kelly, M.D.
St. Paul, Minnesota

BEFORE YOUR BABY ARRIVES

You have to make lots of decisions before your child is born. A couple of the issues you'll need to discuss are outlined below. It's important to read about and discuss these questions yourselves. And, if you schedule a prenatal visit with the physician you've chosen to care for your baby, you'll have a chance to get acquainted and discuss these matters with him or her. A prenatal visit is also a good time to review any complications you may have had during your pregnancy that might require special attention at birth.

Breastfeeding or bottlefeeding. You'll need to decide ahead of time how you plan to feed your baby, since your decision will dictate how you'll need to prepare and what you'll need to buy. See chapter 3 for a full discussion of breastfeeding and bottlefeeding. Should you decide that you are going to breastfeed your child, make sure you read the tips on how to prepare your nipples during the last trimester of your pregnancy (p. 43).

Circumcision. If you have a baby boy, you'll be asked if you want him circumcised or not, a procedure that normally takes place before he leaves the hospital. The American Academy of Pediatrics (AAP) has stated that there are "no valid medical indications for circumcision in the neonatal period." Essentially, it concludes that teaching your son to clean his penis properly will offer him "all the advantages of routine circumcision without the attendant surgical risk." At the same time, the AAP acknowledges that various religious and social factors can play a part in the decision to circumcise or not; it recommends that you discuss all the issues yourselves and then with your physician before your baby is born.

In addition to making decisions on these matters (and probably many others), it's also important to make sure you've got everything you'll need during the first few weeks after your baby is born. You're not likely to have the time or the energy to take shopping trips with a newborn. In various sections of the book, you'll find information to help you make safe, sensible choices. On pp. 35-39, you'll find some recommendations on clothing a new baby; on p. 30, you'll read about outfitting a crib; and on pp. 68-71, you'll learn about what to look for when you buy equipment for your child. Read about car safety on p. 68, and make arrangements before your baby is born to have an approved car seat; be sure his* first trip in a car is as safe as it can be.

*In chapters 1, 3, and 5, we've used feminine pronouns; in chapters 2, 4, and 6, we've used masculine pronouns, except in the step-by-step medical entries, where we alternate masculine and feminine.

Chapter 1

YOUR NEWBORN

I f you're a first-time parent, you've probably been spending lots of time learning about the intricacies of pregnancy and childbirth, practicing your breathing techniques (or coaching your partner), and worrying about how you'll hold up during labor and delivery. You've been concentrating—and rightly so—on the big day, the birth of your child, and preparing to breathe a big sigh of relief when it's over and you're able to hold a healthy baby in your arms.

The memories of your pregnancy and your child's birth will not fade for a long time; in fact, you'll probably sharpen those memories by telling any willing listener the whole story of your labor and delivery in glorious detail. The presence of a newborn, however, immediately puts the experience into a brand-new perspective. The baby that you had gotten used to being "in there" is now "out here." You realize that your pregnancy was just the beginning, not an end in itself. Much lies ahead for both parents and baby.

The year that you're just beginning with your baby will be full of "firsts"— the first smile, the first tooth, the first word, the first step. When you look back over this year, you'll be amazed at how your child has grown and changed, and you should be proud of what you've learned and accomplished. Your baby will need lots of care and attention as she makes the transition from the world inside the womb to the one outside it. And that transition is difficult—for both parents and baby.

CHANGES FOR THE PARENTS

For you as a parent, the birth of your child means, for a start, a great deal less free time, and virtually no "spontaneous" time. You'll have fewer opportunities to go out to a movie or dinner, and such evenings will almost never happen at a moment's notice. You'll find that you need to plan in advance around choosing and "training" sitters and around the baby's schedule, and you'll deliberate far in advance about how long you can be away from home. Once you've walked out the door without your baby (and not without a little trepidation), you'll find yourself thinking and talking of nothing but your child.

No one is going to pretend that a newborn doesn't place a great deal of stress on a couple's relationship—especially if that child is your first. You'll find that even if you share the diapering and bathing and rocking and burping, the entire day *seems* taken up by caring for the baby. And there will be times when child care also seems to consume your entire night as well, as you walk the floor with an infant who hasn't yet figured out the difference between day and night.

Babies are notoriously unpredictable. In the middle of a long-awaited meal, or some too-long-postponed lovemaking, or even a much-needed phone conversation with a supportive friend—suddenly, your baby needs you, and *now*. But if you're like most parents, "demand" is too harsh a word for this. Your baby needs you, so you go, and gladly. There are few things in life more satisfying than your growing confidence in your ability to comfort your child, and to provide the nurturing she needs.

Both parents will know dozens of joys and worries during the first weeks of their baby's life, but it is the mother who is especially vulnerable. In those postpartum days, the tremendous hormonal changes that a woman experiences can contribute to depression, sometimes making it difficult for her to enjoy her newborn as much as she otherwise could. If the child is her first, she's particularly worried about her inexperience (for, if she's like the majority of her peers, she has had precious little exposure to any real-life practice of child-rearing).

If the newborn is not the first child, not only is the mother prone to a bout of "postpartum blues," but she and her spouse will almost inevitably have to contend with a case or two of sibling rivalry. No matter how well you've prepared your older child for the newborn, he still may suffer a slight regression—a normal response to the startling realization that he's no longer the only child. He may suddenly want to take a bottle or start nursing, though he was weaned long ago; his nightly sleep patterns may become disturbed; he may take to sucking his thumb or wetting his pants, even though he showed all signs of being successfully toilet trained. Again, this kind of reaction is common, and is simply your older child's way of requesting the love and attention he's afraid the new arrival will deprive him of.

CHANGES FOR THE BABY

Unquestionably, parents have a great deal of adjusting to do with the birth of their child. But the newborn is also forced to make a transition from the ideal environment of the uterus to the harsher and certainly more varied world outside of her mother's womb. You've probably seen enough photographs of newborns to know that they are generally not the cute, cuddly creatures they will grow to be at three or four months old. Whether your baby was born vaginally or by cesarean, she went through an intense, exhausting physical experience, and she'll need some time to adjust to her new world. In fact, at birth, in response to the exhaustion of the birth process, most newborns enter into a six-hour sleeping period, from which it's difficult to awaken them.

Consider these other facts about newborns:

• A newborn will normally weigh between six and eight pounds (2.7 and 3.6 kg.) and be 18 to 22 inches (45 to 55 cm.) long at birth. Typically, however, she'll lose up to ten percent of her birth weight in the days following birth, then start to regain that weight by the end of her first week.

• Your baby has just spent her entire first nine months of existence passively receiving all of her nourishment through the umbilical cord. She's never had to swallow to appease her hunger—in fact, she's never known what hunger is.

• Before her birth, a newborn has never had to breathe, since she received all of her oxygen through her mother's blood. At birth, although her heart may beat 120 times a minute, her circulation is still sluggish and her breathing is shallow and irregular. She'll also sneeze, gasp, hiccough, and cough. You may think these are cold symptoms, but it's just her way of clearing the mucous from her respiratory system.

• A newborn has never known cold or heat, having been perfectly insulated inside of her mother's body. Her skin has been constantly bathed in amniotic fluid, so she has never felt a rush of air or a sharp poke. At birth, however, her temperature drops rapidly in response to the outside air, and great care must be taken to keep her warm.

• While she was in the womb, all outside sound was muffled for her by layers of fluid, blood, and tissue, so she's been ignorant of sharp, loud noises. Her sleeping and waking schedule has been entirely her own, since she has had no need to distinguish between day and night. And the most constant, familiar movement she has known, as she has been lodged in the cradle of her mother's body, has been the gentle rocking created by her mother's daily movements.

It's no wonder, then, that a newborn may take a few weeks to adjust. She's just been born into a world in which she suddenly needs to eat and defecate and breathe, and is expected to sleep on schedule and be cuddled and held and cooed to. In spite of all that babies go through to survive, and all that parents must do and experience in order to help them survive, the first year of life is a marvelous adventure. Babies *do* thrive, and the love of their parents never ceases to grow.

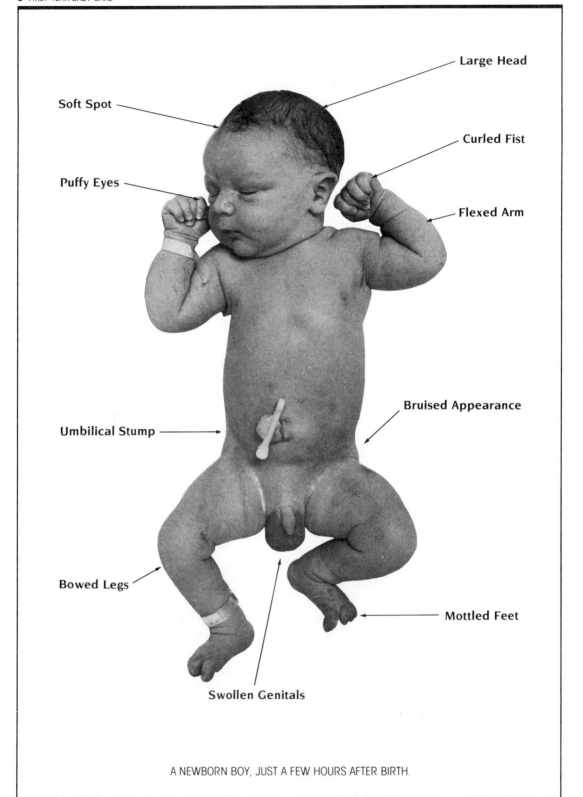

Large Head

Soft Spot

Curled Fist

Puffy Eyes

Flexed Arm

Bruised Appearance

Umbilical Stump

Bowed Legs

Mottled Feet

Swollen Genitals

A NEWBORN BOY, JUST A FEW HOURS AFTER BIRTH.

CHARACTERISTICS OF A NEWBORN

Head

The head of a newborn may look lopsided and may still be molded into a pointy melon shape by the pressures of the birth canal (although some babies delivered by cesarean do not have molding). It will also seem large in proportion to her body (it's about one-fourth of the body length). The two soft spots (called *fontanels*) are covered by a tough membrane where the bones of the skull have not yet fused. (The anterior fontanel, the larger one at the top near the front, closes at 18 to 24 months. The posterior fontanel, at the top near the back, closes by six months.) A newborn's neck is usually short and creased.

It's impossible to predict how much hair a newborn will have or keep. Some newborns have no hair or a short crop that will fall out and be replaced around six weeks. Others have lots and may never lose it.

Face

A newborn's eyes will probably be red and puffy from the pressures of birth and from drops or ointment that may have been used. Her eyes will usually be blue-gray in color (brown in dark-skinned babies), and permanent color won't develop until about six months. Tears may be present from birth, but don't appear in most babies until six weeks or so.

The nose of a newborn, which is entirely made of cartilage, appears flat and broad. Also, her cheeks are usually fat, and she'll seem to have almost no chin.

Skin

The skin of a newborn is wrinkled and loose, and it may look dry and start peeling after a few days. A newborn's body *may* be covered with *vernix caseosa*, a white, waxy substance that has eased the baby's movement through the birth canal. Her body may still have *lanugo*, a downy fuzz over the shoulders, back, and cheeks; this disappears within a few weeks.

The color of her skin usually fluctuates for the first few days, ranging from purplish-blue to pink or grayish. Babies of Black, Asian or Mediterranean parents often have light skin at first.

Body

The abdomen of a newborn is large, her hips are small, and her body curls inward. An umbilical stump is present where the umbilical cord has been cut from the navel. The stump will dry up and fall off on its own between ten and fourteen days after birth. (See pp. 28-29 for how to care for a newborn's navel.)

The breasts and genitalia of a newborn may be swollen in both sexes due to the presence of hormones from the mother, and baby girls may bleed slightly from the vagina. This swelling disappears in three to five days. Urine and stool will usually appear within the first 24 hours. (See p. 18.)

Arms

A newborn's arms are flexed, and her hands are curled into fists. Her hands will generally be cool and may look blue because of her immature circulatory system. Her wrists may be fat and creased, and her fingernails may be long and sharp. (See p. 29 for how to trim an infant's fingernails.)

Legs

The knees of a newborn are bent and her legs are bowed. Like her hands, a newborn's feet may look mottled and bluish because of her immature circulatory system, and they may appear flat because of fat pads on the soles.

CONDITIONS THAT MAY BE PRESENT AT BIRTH

Birthmarks

Some birthmarks may be present at birth, while others may develop in the first month of life. This is very common and should be no reason for concern. Most birthmarks will disappear or fade on their own by the time your child is of school age.

Blisters

You may notice a blister on your baby's upper lip, caused by intense sucking.

Broken clavicle (collar bone)

A newborn may be born with a fractured collar bone that's incurred during the birth; it will heal completely with time.

Dislocated hips

Dislocated hips are also fairly common in newborns. The condition can be treated in various ways by your physician.

Hematoma

A hematoma is a swelling of fluid beneath the scalp, caused by pressure of the baby's head against the pelvic outlet. Your newborn may have several that look like big "goose eggs," but don't worry—they disappear in about a week.

Milia

Milia are undeveloped or blocked sweat glands that may show up as white, pinpoint spots on the nose, chin, and cheeks. They disappear over time.

Newborn jaundice

Jaundice refers to the yellow color in the baby's skin, a condition that often appears within a few days of birth and disappears within a week. This is a normal process and should not be a cause for concern. This yellow color is caused by *bilirubin*, a by-product of the breakdown of red blood cells in the newborn. All of us have "old" red blood cells that break down, but newborns have more of them and their immature livers are somewhat slow in processing the bilirubin.

Only rarely is newborn jaundice a cause for concern. If it is, your physician will monitor the level of bilirubin with blood tests after birth. If it persists beyond five to seven days of birth, further evaluation may be necessary, and if the skin becomes jaundiced to a fair degree, it may be necessary to treat the condition by putting the newborn under "bilirubin lights." Also, about five percent of breastfed babies have prolonged jaundice, probably because of the fatty acids in breast milk. A temporary interruption of nursing will abruptly decrease the level of bilirubin. You can then resume breastfeeding, and even though the level of bilirubin will rise, you needn't be concerned.

Newborn rash

Before they are a few days old, many newborns are affected by a rash. Splotches or pimples often appear on the chest, back, or face and disappear without treatment.

Tongue tie

The fold of the skin attaching the tongue to the base of the mouth may be longer and thicker than usual, inhibiting the tongue's forward movement. This condition needs no correction and will not lead to eating or speech problems.

Wrist lesions

These are produced by fetal sucking and will disappear.

NEWBORN EXAMS

Your newborn will undergo a variety of tests in the hospital. Some take place immediately after birth and some are delayed until right before you're discharged from the hospital, when your infant is more "settled." All of these tests are routine and are no cause for alarm.

Apgar tests

Immediately after your baby is born, a doctor or nurse will evaluate her using the Apgar scale (see below), which provides an indication of your baby's well-being. The doctor or nurse will observe the newborn's heart rate, respiratory effort, muscle tone, reflex irritability (or response), and skin color, and will record a score of 0 to 2 for each of these five areas (so the maximum is 10). Readings are recorded at one minute and then again at five minutes after birth. Don't be overly concerned about your baby's performance here, since a perfect score of 10 is unusual, and scores over 7 are perfectly okay.

Sign	0	1	2
Heart Rate	Absent	Slow (below 100 beats/min.)	Over 100 beats/min.
Respiratory Effort	Absent	Slow, irregular	Good, crying
Muscle Tone	Limp, flaccid	Some flexing of extremities	Active motion
Reflex Irritability			
1. Response to slap on foot	No response	Weak cry or grimace	Rigorous cry
2. Response to catheter in nostril	No response	Grimace	Cough or sneeze
Color	Blue, pale	Body pink, extremities blue	Completely pink

Newborn exam

A physician will examine your baby thoroughly, usually within 24 hours of your baby's birth and then again prior to discharge. Try to make arrangements to be present at one of these exams, since it will give you a good opportunity to ask questions and learn more about your baby. The doctor will check your baby from head to toe, listen to her heartbeat, feel her pulse, look for dislocated hips, test her reflexes (see pp. 12-13) and examine the inner organs that can be felt through her soft skin. It's also possible at this time for the examining physician to determine more exactly what your baby's gestational age is.

Screening tests

Three or four days after birth, newborns are tested for three diseases that have no visible signs but could cause mental retardation *if untreated*. A few drops of blood are taken from the baby's heel and then tested for these diseases:

• **Phenylketonuria (PKU).** PKU, which occurs in one infant in 15,000, is a hereditary disease that causes mental retardation. Carried by parents who are not affected by the disease themselves, PKU is caused by the body's inability to digest protein normally. Treatment consists of putting the baby on a special diet that's low in phenylalanine, the part of the protein that the body can't digest.

• **Galactosemia.** Galactosemia, which is also carried by parents who are not affected by the disease, occurs in one infant in 60,000. It occurs when the body cannot use milk sugar (lactose) normally, and it can cause mental retardation, cataracts, and an enlarged liver. It is treated by a diet that avoids milk products.

• **Hypothyroidism.** Hypothyroidism, which occurs in one infant in 5,000 and causes mental retardation and lethargy, is most often caused by a defect in the development of the thyroid gland. It's treated by thyroid hormone medication.

YOUR NEWBORN'S WORLD

Until fairly recently, scientists thought that newborns were naturally passive and uninvolved with their surroundings—little "blank tablets" waiting for the world to form them. Today, researchers are finding ways to discover what is going on inside the heads of newborns, and they are learning that newborns are remarkably responsive and complete little people. They perceive the world almost as well as adults, and they're keenly interested in it—especially the people in it. The more newborns are studied, the more extraordinary they prove to be.

Here's a brief description of how a newborn's senses and other faculties function at birth.

Touch

Newborns are exceptionally aware of touch, probably more so than adults. Touch has been called "almost a language" for infants, who readily perceive small changes in texture or temperature. More than any other sense, touch allows a developing baby to relate to its surroundings before birth, which is why it is such an important sense early in life.

Newborns react with pleasure to warm, soft, firm pressure, especially on the front surfaces of their bodies. Holding them closely or swaddling them (see how on pp. 16-17) will often calm them. Recent research indicates that close physical contact between mother and child in the first weeks of life is very important to the newborn's sense of well-being. In fact, the *bonding* that takes place between the mother and her newborn in the first hours of life is not only desirable, but might aid the baby's development in ways that can be measured several years afterward.

Recognizing the importance of parent-infant bonding, many childbearing couples want to spend as much time as they can with their newborn immediately after birth. And hospitals are relaxing the routines that used to interfere with this kind of interaction. Cuddling, kissing, touching, lots of eye-to-eye and skin-to-skin contact, and other physical manifestations of affection are a wonderful way for both parents to begin their relationship with their baby right away, and the mother who chooses to breastfeed her baby can begin to establish that special relationship with her child within hours of birth.

Sight

Although newborns can see from the moment of birth, they are extremely nearsighted. Their eyes are like simple cameras with the focus fixed at about 8 to 12 inches (20 to 30 cm.). That is the distance, not coincidentally, between a mother's and a newborn's face when the baby is being cuddled or nursed. Beyond that distance, newborns perceive only brightness and movement. They can track an object moving slowly from side to side and, with more difficulty, an object moving up and down.

Babies observe the world with limited vision but unlimited interest. Newborns will drop their mother's nipple in the delivery room to stare at an attractive object. Shortly after birth, babies are most attracted by complex, highly patterned, visual objects. Within weeks, though, they would rather look at faces than anything else. (To a newborn, an object is a face if it is round and has a hairline, eyes, and a mouth.)

Note: By two months, your baby should "track" objects that move slowly in front of her line of sight. If you have any concerns about your baby's sight, raise them with your physician. Babies can be tested even as newborns, if there's any reason to suspect a problem. Crossed eyes, however, are normal during the early part of infancy (see p. 107).

Hearing

Babies are born with a well-developed sense of hearing. Within ten minutes after birth, they can locate the source of a sound. They seem to respond to sounds lasting ten seconds, but not to sounds lasting only a second or two. Newborns seem so intrigued by sounds even at birth that they will discontinue sucking to pay better attention to an attractive sound. Just moments after birth, newborns will seem to display definite preferences in sounds. They especially like high-pitched voices and sounds that are rhythmic and soft.

Note: An infant should move or "startle" (see p. 12) in response to a loud noise. If you have any questions about your child's hearing, raise them with your physician. See Hearing Loss, p. 115.

Smell and taste

The senses of smell and taste are essentially the same for infants. Less is known about what babies can smell and taste than about their other senses, primarily because researchers find it difficult to tell when a baby is discriminating between one smell or taste and another. Newborns *do* react to sweet, sour, and salty tastes. They are obviously upset by foul odors. And they can differentiate among plain, slightly sweetened, and very sweet water.

Intelligence

Babies are born knowing little or nothing. They seem to lack specificity in responses—meaning that they react with an identical response (such as finger sucking) to a wide variety of stimuli. A single change in a newborn's environment, such as a drop in temperature, will often cause its whole body to react. Newborns have such short memories that objects are not remembered unless they reappear within two-and-a-half seconds.

Yet babies are anything but intellectually passive. Their interest in their surroundings is keen and discriminating. They can choose to pay attention to a single object in their environment. Even when they are quite young, babies can combine touch, sight, and hearing into meaningful patterns.

Sociability

Most remarkably, babies seem "programmed" to take an interest in the people who surround them, although they are born knowing nothing about the existence of other beings. Newborns crave contact—by touch, sight, smell, and hearing—with people, especially their parents. By one week they might recognize the sound of a parent's voice, and by two weeks they can know their parents, especially their primary caregivers, by sight. Babies only four weeks old will behave differently with their parents than with other people.

NEWBORN REFLEXES

A newborn's reflexes are her spontaneous, automatic responses to external or internal stimuli. They are the building blocks of intelligence and the foundation of physical coordination. Some reflexes, like the gagging and blinking responses, remain through life. Others, like the grasping and walking reflexes, disappear, or "go underground," only to re-emerge later as consciously controlled activities. The physician who examines your baby will check for the presence of some of these reflexes as indications of a healthy nervous system.

REFLEXES THAT DISAPPEAR

Name	Description	What triggers it	Disappearance
Startle (Moro)	Your baby flings out her arms and legs, then quickly pulls them into her chest while her body curls as if to cling.	External stimuli like sudden changes in light, noise, movement or position. Internal stimuli like the baby's own crying or muscle twitches during sleep.	It tapers off in 1 to 2 weeks and disappears by 6 months.
Sucking	Your baby puckers her lips and grasps, while her tongue curls inward to pull.	Touching a part of the baby's mouth or cheek with a nipple or finger.	It's strongest in the first 4 months. After 6 months it fades, merging gradually with conscious activity.
Rooting	Your baby turns her head in the direction of the stroking and searches with her lips for a nipple. Used to seek food.	Stroking a cheek or an area around the mouth.	It continues while baby is nursing.
Grasp	Your baby's fingers curl as if to hold on to an object; or her toes curl.	Stroking the hands or pressing the ball of the feet at the base of the toes.	It decreases noticeably after 10 days and usually disappears around 4 months. May continue in the feet until 8 months.
Stepping	Your baby lifts each foot in turn as if to walk.	Holding her in a standing position, pressing down a little.	It diminishes after 1 week and will disappear in about 2 months.
Placing	Your baby tries to step upwards to put her feet on the surface of a table or bed.	Holding her shins in contact with an edge.	It disappears in about 2 months.
Tonic neck	Your baby's head is turned to one side, her body is arched. She extends one arm straight out and flexes the other arm in a "fencer's pose."	Laying your baby on her back.	It's most obvious at 2 to 3 months and disappears at around 4 months.

PERMANENT REFLEXES

Name	Description	What triggers it	Disappearance
Blinking	Your baby's eyelids open and close rapidly.	Bright light, touching eyelid, sudden noise.	_____
Gag	Your baby chokes, gasps, spits up, and may turn blue. (Even when her head is under water, the reflex in most cases prevents breathing in water.)	Foreign matter in respiratory system.	_____
Swallowing	Your baby's trachea closes, while her esophagus opens.	Food in the mouth.	_____
Withdrawal	Your baby tries to pull away, drawing her limbs close to her body.	Pain, cold air.	_____
"Parachute"	Your baby extends her hands out to protect herself.	"Diving" your baby toward the floor.	_____

Chapter 2

DAILY CARE FOR YOUR BABY

As you go about your daily routine of bathing your baby, changing his diapers, dressing and undressing him, comforting him when he's fussy, and putting him to sleep, you'll have many occasions to reflect on his complete dependence on the adults who take care of him. This dependence won't change much during the first year. Left alone, your child will be just as incapable of changing his own diaper at one year of age as he was at one week.

Before you change your first diaper, you're liable to feel just as helpless as your baby. You'll be nervous—especially if you're being observed by a well-meaning but intrusive friend or relative—and each movement will seem awkward and unnatural. The diaper you put on your baby may leak because it's too loose, bath-time may give you the shakes, and dressing your infant for his first outing may seem to require a minimum of four hands.

The purpose of this chapter is to get you through this early stage. With the instructions here (which you may only have to refer to once), plus lots of practice, you'll soon be able to change diapers in your sleep (in fact, you probably will once in a while). And along with the basic skills, you'll develop a great deal of patience, the dexterity necessary to do more than one thing at a time, and the resourcefulness required to amuse a baby who's undergoing his umpteenth diaper change.

Once you can relax at these tasks, you'll come to know the real joys of meeting your baby's basic needs. What's so satisfying about the daily care of your baby is that it gives both mothers and fathers the chance to establish a special relationship with their child. Bathing and diapering allow you to hold and make plenty of eye contact with your baby, to sing special songs, and to play silly games. And rocking your baby to sleep can be one of the most blissful moments of your day. These are the private moments that only parents know.

HANDLING YOUR BABY

WHAT YOU NEED TO KNOW

• *About holding your baby*: A healthy baby is not as fragile as he may seem to you, so don't be afraid to touch and hold him. Even the "soft spots" on his head are not really soft; their sturdy membranes are designed to protect your baby's head from physical shocks, such as falling. You may even notice a pulsing of veins under the surface, but don't worry, this is normal. Try to cuddle, rock and talk to your baby as often as possible. He needs to be touched and held often in order to feel physically and emotionally comfortable and secure. Don't worry about "spoiling" a child for many months yet.

• *About picking up your baby*: It's important to support your baby's head when you're picking him up and laying him down during the early months. Until the third or fourth

month, his neck is too weak and his head is too heavy to hold steady by himself. If you're *gradual* and *gentle* in your movements, you're also less likely to startle him unnecessarily.

• *About swaddling your baby*: During the first three or four months, most babies like being fairly tightly wrapped in a receiving blanket or shawl. Swaddling provides warmth and the sensation of constant touch. It helps quiet a baby for sleep, so it's a particularly good way to soothe a "colicky" baby (especially when you combine it with rocking).

• *About rocking your baby*: Since rocking recreates the motion your baby felt during his prenatal state, it can help soothe an irritable baby and quiet him for sleep. Don't rock too slowly, however. About 60 rocks per minute is a good rhythm.

HOLDING YOUR BABY

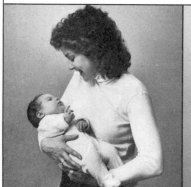

Cradled in your arms.

With the baby's head nestled against your shoulder while you support his back with one hand and his bottom with the other.

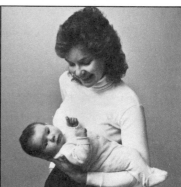

Using the "football" carry. Lay the baby along one of your arms, close to your side, cradling his head with your hand.

HANDLING YOUR BABY

PICKING UP YOUR BABY

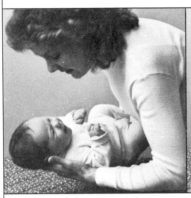  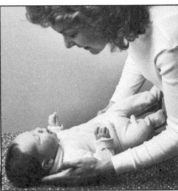

If he's lying on his back: Slide one hand under his neck and fan out your fingers to support his head. Bend down so that you can comfortably slide your other arm under him. Lift him slowly in a compact bundle. Don't let his arms and legs dangle.

If he's lying on his stomach: Put one arm under your baby's shoulder and neck. Support his head with your hand. Slide your other arm under his middle and fan your fingers to support his trunk and thighs. Lift him slowly in a compact bundle.

To put your baby down: Lower his head and back to the mattress, keeping your arms under him. Be especially careful to support his head as you lower it. Lower his bottom, then gently slide both your arms from underneath his body.

SWADDLING YOUR BABY

 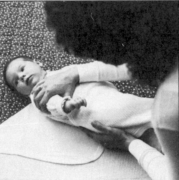 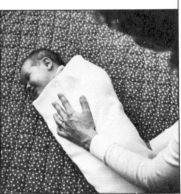

1 Lay the blanket in front of you in a diamond shape, with a point at the top. Fold down the top point. Lay your baby on his back on the blanket so that his head is just above the edge you've just folded down.

2 Take up one of the side points of the blanket and pull it firmly over the baby's chest, tucking it under his thighs. Then bring the bottom point up over his feet.

3 Take up the other side and stretch it over the baby in the opposite direction. Tuck it under his thighs. Early on, you'll probably want to confine his arms, but later you'll want to make sure that his fingers are free for sucking.

ELIMINATION

URINATION

The newborn

Don't be surprised if your newborn always seems to have a wet diaper. It's very normal for a newborn to urinate as often as thirty times a day. But a very young baby who stays dry for four to six hours may be dehydrated (see p. 109) or have a urinary obstruction (see p. 126) and should be taken to the doctor.

The first year

Once your baby's older, he should have at least six to eight wet diapers a day. If he has fewer, make sure he's getting enough liquid. In especially hot weather, it's okay to supplement his breast milk or formula with water or unsweetened fruit juice. If the problem persists, see a doctor.

BOWEL MOVEMENTS

Right after birth

A greenish-black, tarlike substance called *meconium* builds up in a baby's intestines before he is born. After birth, it must be passed out before normal digestion can take place. Generally, the intestines are free of meconium by the second or third day of your baby's life (or before he leaves the hospital). If your child is born at home and fails to eliminate the meconium by the third day, consult your doctor. His bowels may be obstructed.

The early weeks

As your baby adjusts to getting his nourishment from the breast or bottle (rather than from his mother's placenta), his digestive system will need some time to adapt. At first, his stools will probably be very frequent (after every feeding or even more often) with a loose, curd-like texture. The color may vary from bright green to green-brown to golden, and the fecal matter may be expelled quite violently. These are all normal features of your baby's early days, and none of them suggest your baby has diarrhea as long as he seems content and is feeding well. (See p. 111 for more on diarrhea.) By the time he's three weeks old, his stools will take on predictable characteristics and his movements will be less frequent.

The first year

The breastfed baby. The stools of a breastfed baby are mild smelling, mustard yellow, and creamy. Greenish or brownish stools or movements with a "seedy" or watery consistency are not uncommon and are no sign of an intestinal disturbance as long as your baby seems content in every other way. Since breast milk is so perfectly suited to your baby, it's almost impossible for him to become constipated as long as your milk is his sole source of nutrition. (See p. 103 for more on constipation.) Don't worry if your baby goes for several days without a bowel movement (even if he does strain a bit when he finally passes one), as long as the texture is still soft. A frequency rate of several a day to one every several days is considered normal. And it's normal for him to adjust his pattern often. As long as he's thriving, don't worry.

The bottlefed baby. The stools of a bottlefed baby are generally more solid than those of a breastfed baby, because there is more waste for him to get rid of. They tend to be light brown or golden in color and they are likely to smell more like ordinary adult stools. The bottlefed baby can have as many as six movements a day in his early weeks, but then as few as one a day (and sometimes one every few days) as he matures. The important thing to watch is the consistency. In the unlikely event that his formula is not perfectly suited to him, the first sign of this will appear in his stools.

When solids are introduced. Introducing anything new to your baby's digestive system may cause a change in the appearance or the smell of his stools. The stools may take on the actual color of any new solid food you give your baby—orange after eating carrots, greenish after peas, and red after beets.

A note about messes

Changing diapers will probably never be your favorite activity. Diapers will leak, clothing will get soiled, you may even get wet from time to time when your baby urinates in the middle of a diaper change. Try to keep your humor about all of this. Don't make your child feel that he's done something distasteful when he urinates or has a bowel movement. He has no control over either the frequency or the manner of movements, and he won't have any control for a couple of years.

TYPES OF DIAPER CARE

Whether you decide to buy disposable diapers, wash your own, or use a diaper service will depend on a number of factors—your schedule, your budget, your baby's reaction to various kinds of diapers. The chart below lists some of the advantages and disadvantages of each method.

	ADVANTAGES	DISADVANTAGES
Washing your own diapers	• Offers the most inexpensive way of providing diapers for your baby. • Offers flexibility—cotton squares can be folded and refolded to fit your baby as he grows.	• Is time-consuming—you have to soak, wash, rinse, dry, and often fold diapers before they're ready for use. • Can be inconvenient when you're traveling. • Requires that you use plastic pants, which can increase the likelihood of diaper rash.
Using disposable diapers	• Offers convenience. • Is especially handy for traveling and visiting. • Eliminates safety pins that may injure your child.	• Costs at least twice as much as caring for your own diapers. • Demands frequent trips to the store to maintain your supply. • May cause diaper rash because the plastic outer liners prevent air circulation.
Using a diaper service	• Saves time. Extremely convenient when you have a newborn. • Is less expensive than using disposables. • Uses special disinfectant soaps.	• Is more expensive than washing your own diapers. • Makes it necessary for someone to be home when diapers are to be picked up and dropped off.

DIAPERS AND OTHER NECESSITIES

Disposable diapers

Disposable diapers have a plastic outer liner to keep moisture in, an inner layer of absorbent paper, and an inner plastic lining that keeps moisture away from your baby's skin. Disposables come equipped with adhesive fasteners in place of pins. Some brands have elastic around the legs for added protection against leaking. Have lots on hand to start with, since you'll probably use 80 to 100 a week with a newborn.

Cloth diapers

Cloth diapers are usually made out of gauze or cotton flannel. They're generally quick drying and very absorbent, and they come *prefolded* or *unfolded*. You'll probably need three to four dozen to start with.

• **Prefolded diapers** come with an extra thickness down the center for added absorbency, so they don't need to be folded. This saves time, but also makes them less flexible in size.

• **Unfolded diapers** need to be folded in any of the ways shown below.

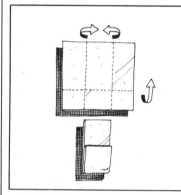 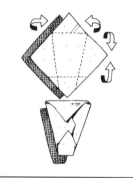 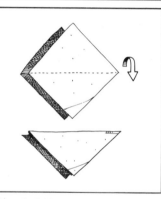

Rectangular fold

Depending on the size of your baby, fold the diaper in halves or thirds. Then fold the bottom third up and use it for extra absorbency in the back for a girl and in the front for a boy.

Kite fold

Make the diaper into a square and position it as a diamond in front of you. Fold the top point down part way, then fold the two side corners over. Finally, fold the bottom point up, and you're ready to use it just as you would use a rectangular diaper.

Triangle fold

Fold the diaper in half from point to point, making a double-thickness triangle. This is especially good for boys or larger babies.

Waterproof pants

Plastic pants have elastic around the waist and legs to prevent your baby's clothing from becoming soaked with urine. They allow no drying or air circulation, however, so they can be responsible for diaper rash on sensitive skin. Some babies, however, can wear them day and night with no ill effect. When you use plastic pants, make sure they completely cover the diaper to prevent his clothing from getting wet. Waterproof pants usually come in small, medium, large, and extra large sizes. Have three or four pair of small pants on hand to start with.

Diaper liners

Diaper liners are disposable squares that you can place inside cloth diapers to hold the bulk of a baby's stool. Using them means you'll have to do less work scraping diapers.

Changing table   Any waist-high surface will do. Various commercial changing tables are available, of course, or you can convert an old dresser into a perfectly usable surface. Just make sure that it's covered with something soft—a foam pad or a baby carriage mattress works well. Cover *that* with a removable and washable flannel cloth. For additional protection, you may want to keep a small square of cotton-covered rubber sheeting under your baby's bottom when you change him. Put up a shelf nearby so everything you need will be within reach. It's also wise to attach a strap to the table, since some babies are so wiggly you'll want that extra measure of safety.

DIAPER CARE

Soaking cloth diapers   To soak dirty diapers properly, you'll need a covered, deodorized diaper pail and a soaking bleach or diaper sterilizer. Partially fill the diaper pail with water and ½ to 1 cup (125 to 250 ml.) of soaking bleach or diaper sterilizer (follow the instructions on the package). Then, when you remove a dirty diaper from your baby, here's what you do:

- If the diaper is simply wet, it's a good idea to first rinse it, then wring it out, and drop it in the diaper pail.
- If the diaper is soiled, scrape, shake or scrub the stool into the toilet, and then rinse the diaper in the toilet or the sink until the stain is well faded. Then drop the diaper into the pail.

It's best if your diapers have soaked in the disinfecting solution for at least six hours before you wash them. If you plan to wash diapers but have a few that haven't soaked for six hours, keep them in a plastic bag and simply add them to the next pailful.

Washing and drying cloth diapers   **Washing**. When you're ready to wash diapers, put them in a sink and let the soaking solution drain from them before you put them in the washing machine. Or you can put the diapers in your washing machine and run the spin cycle to drain out the soaking solution; then add soap and begin the wash cycle.

Wash diapers with a mild soap in a machine on the hottest cycle possible, with at least two rinses. If your baby suffers from diaper rash or has very sensitive skin, you may need to run an extra rinse cycle. (You can also throw waterproof plastic pants in a washing machine, but they should not be put in a dryer.)

Drying. Either tumble-dry or line-dry your diapers. If you use a dryer, be aware that the scented paper squares that eliminate static or soften fabrics contain chemicals that might irritate sensitive skin. If you dry your diapers on the line, but can't do it outside, they may become stiff. You'll then have to use a fabric softener in the rinse, but be sure it's rinsed out completely so it doesn't irritate your baby's skin.

Disposable diapers   The great convenience of disposable diapers, of course, is that you can just throw them away when they're dirty or wet. You should know, however, that the inner absorbent material of a disposable, which holds most of the urine or stool, is biodegradable and can be flushed down the toilet. Do not flush either the inner plastic lining or the waterproof outer layer.

DIAPERING YOUR BABY

WHAT YOU NEED TO KNOW

● It's best to change your baby after every bowel movement and whenever he becomes fairly wet—this usually adds up to ten to twelve changes a day. You don't have to be obsessive about this, however. Since babies urinate a lot, you'll drive yourself crazy if you try to keep up.

● Unless he has an especially bad case of diaper rash, you don't need to change your baby's diapers during the night. If he's sleeping peacefully, you can be sure he's comfortable. He won't be chilled if he's covered and the wet diapers aren't exposed to air.

● See p. 110 for how to treat diaper rash.

● Keep your hands dry and oil-free when you're using disposables or the plastic tabs might not stick. (If they *don't* stick, use masking tape to secure the diaper.)

● If your baby wets a great deal at night while he's asleep, or if you don't want to rouse him to change him after a drowsy, middle-of-the-night feeding, double-diaper him before his last evening feeding, using two diapers in place of one.

● If your baby's navel hasn't yet healed, fold the front edge of the diaper *below* the navel, so it can't chafe and irritate that tender area.

● Don't ever turn your back on a baby lying on a changing table—even a newborn can wriggle and fall to the floor.

WHAT YOU NEED

Diapers, diaper pins and waterproof pants (if you're using cloth diapers), cotton balls or washcloth, warm water, diaper rash ointment (see p. 110). Commercial baby wipes, which are convenient but expensive, are fine to use as long as your baby has no reaction to them.

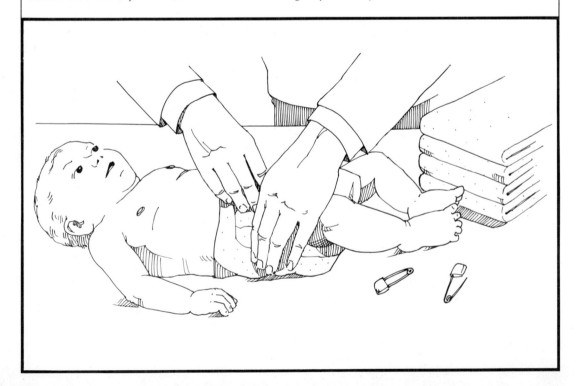

WHAT TO DO

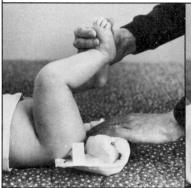
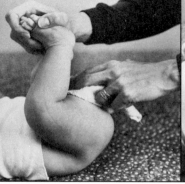

1 Place your baby on his back on a changing table or other convenient, flat surface. Unpin the used diaper and remove it. If the diaper is soiled, roll it toward your baby so it is sure to hold in all of the stool. With the unsoiled end of the diaper, clean any clinging stool off your baby's bottom.

2 Holding your baby's legs, lift his bottom up and finish the cleaning with a warm, damp washcloth, always wiping from front to back. If the diaper was simply wet, you needn't wash your baby. Then always allow your baby's bottom to air dry. Apply a doctor-recommended ointment or lotion if he has diaper rash.

3 Lift his bottom up again and place the fresh diaper (cloth or disposable) beneath, with the top edge of the diaper at waist level. (When you're using disposables, make sure the tape tabs are behind your baby.) Fold over any extra material in front for a boy or in back for a girl.

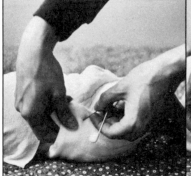

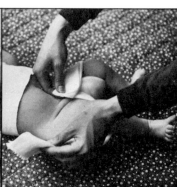

4a **For rectangular diapers (cloth):** Bring the center portion of the rectangle up over the baby's front and then pin the diapers securely at each side. The back should overlap the front. Be sure to put your own hand between the diaper and your baby's skin to avoid sticking him.

4b **For rectangular diapers (disposable):** Bring the center portion of the rectangle up over the baby's front and then tape the diapers securely at each side. The back should overlap the front.

4c **For triangular diapers:** Bring the point up between the baby's legs, fold it down, and hold it in place with one hand while you fold one side in to meet it. Hold both points in place while you bring over the third point. Pin all three points at the center, making sure you put your hand between the diaper and your baby's skin to avoid sticking him.

BATHING YOUR BABY (SPONGE BATHS)

WHAT YOU NEED TO KNOW

• It is generally recommended that you sponge bathe your baby *until* his umbilical cord has fallen off and his navel has fully healed. If your child has been circumcised, sponge bathe him until his penis has fully healed. (The circumcision usually heals before the cord falls off.)

• You needn't bathe or shampoo your child every day. Two or three times a week is often enough as long as you keep his face and genital area clean. More frequent shampooings could cause a dry, scaly scalp.

• Newborns sometimes fear being completely naked, so if your baby seems annoyed during his bath, you might try uncovering and washing only one part of him at a time.

• Some babies don't like to lie still or stay quiet long enough for a complete sponge bath, so you can do it one step at a time throughout the day (for instance, when you're changing him).

WHAT YOU NEED

A bowl of warm water; a soft washcloth; cotton balls; gentle, unscented soap; a soft towel; cotton swabs; rubbing alcohol; a sponge cushion (optional).

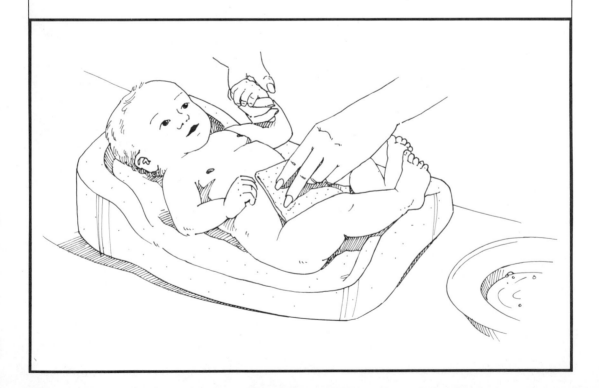

WHAT TO DO

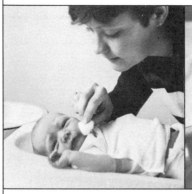
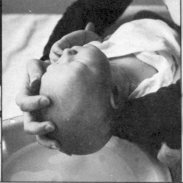
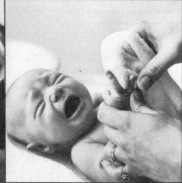

1 Without undressing your baby, place him on a sponge cushion or a changing table. Starting with his head, wipe each eye with a separate sterile cotton ball moistened with warm water. Wipe from the inside of the eye outwards. With another moistened cotton ball, wipe around your baby's ears. Continue with a damp cloth to clean around his mouth, chin, and neck.

2 Hold your baby's head over a bowl of water and gently wet his scalp. Then shampoo it with a mild soap, making sure you massage it gently with your fingertips, not your fingernails. Rinse his head and pat it dry.

3 Remove his shirt and gently wash his chest and arms, making sure you get at all the creases in his skin, including those around his neck. Wipe his hands, checking for lint in between his fingers. Also look for long or sharp fingernails (see p. 29 for how to trim fingernails). Rinse him with clean, warm water and pat dry.

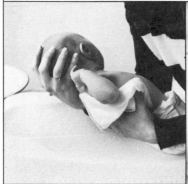
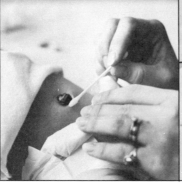
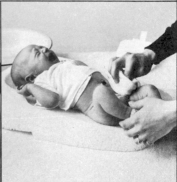

4 While supporting his head, gently turn your baby on his side, and wash and rinse his back. Pat dry and dress his top half.

5 While it's still healing, wipe the navel with a cotton swab soaked in rubbing alcohol, cleaning it right down to the base. Avoid wetting the navel area until it has completely healed.

6 Remove your baby's diaper and then gently soap and rinse the genital area, buttocks, legs, and feet. Gently and thoroughly pat dry. Apply a doctor-recommended ointment if your baby has a rash. Diaper and dress your baby.

BATHING YOUR BABY (TUB BATHS)

WHAT YOU NEED TO KNOW

• It is generally advised that you don't bathe your baby in a tub until his umbilical cord has fallen off and his navel has *fully* healed. If your child has been circumcised, wait until his penis has completely healed before giving him a tub bath.

• As noted earlier, you needn't bathe or shampoo your child every day. Two or three times a week is often enough as long as you keep his face and genital area clean.

• It is safest to use a mild, unscented soap. Any disinfectant or highly perfumed soap may be irritating to the skin and cause dryness and rashes.

• Your baby may not initially like a full bath. Don't worry and don't force him. Continue sponge bathing until he's a little older, and remember that most babies eventually have a great time in their bath. Don't rush and you'll both soon be enjoying it.

• You should never turn your back on your baby or leave him alone in the tub, no matter how short a time and how little water you're using. If you must leave him to answer the phone, quickly wrap him in a towel and put him on the floor.

WHAT YOU NEED

A portable baby tub with sponge cushion (a plastic dish tub will work for a smaller baby); a table or counter top at a convenient height; a soft washcloth; soft, unscented soap; a soft towel; baby shampoo.

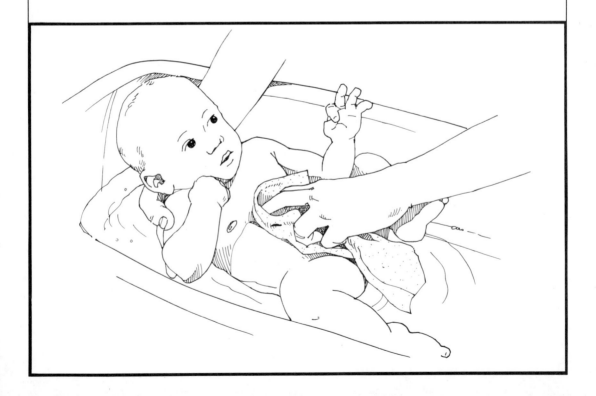

WHAT TO DO

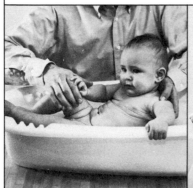

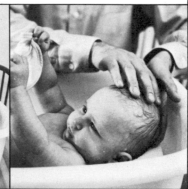

1 Run about 2 inches (5 cm.) of water in the tub and then check the water temperature to make sure it's pleasantly warm. Extreme temperatures can scald, burn, or shock a baby. Undress your baby and gently lower him into the tub, easing his bottom in first.

2 Using a soft washcloth and gentle soap, start by washing your baby's face, ears, and neck, paying special attention to the folds of skin under the chin.

3 Shampoo his head, working from front to back so that the soap doesn't get into his eyes. Scrub his scalp well, using the tips of your fingers, not your fingernails. (Don't worry about the "soft spot" on his head—it's tough.) Rinse well.

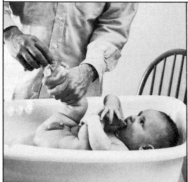

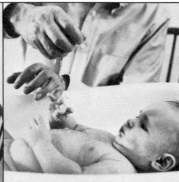

4 Soap up the rest of your baby's body, looking carefully for pieces of lint that tend to lodge between fingers and toes and in creases of flesh. Lift his legs, and wash and rinse the genitals just as you would any other part of the body, but do so after you've washed his face.

5 Then help your baby sit up while you wash and rinse his back. (An older baby, of course, will be able to sit up without support.)

6 Rinse your baby well to prevent irritation from soap residue. Lift him from the tub and wrap him in a large, soft, warm towel. Pat, don't rub, him dry. Apply a doctor-recommended ointment if your baby has a rash. Diaper and dress your baby.

THE BIG TUB

WHAT YOU NEED TO KNOW

• Your child is probably ready for bathing in a standard bathtub by the time he's able to sit up steadily unsupported, and certainly by the time he's too big for his infant tub.

• To eliminate the risk of a possible drowning or even an unintentional dunking, be sure to run only a few inches of water in the tub for your baby's bath.

• Always test the bath water before you put your baby in—it should be mildly warm to the touch. Try to keep your child away from the faucets during the bath—one playful turn of the hot water and he could scald himself.

Run a little cold water last so that if your child touches the faucet it won't burn him.

• At first, you may want to bathe with your child to make sure he doesn't slip and bump himself. This also saves you the trouble of kneeling on a hard tile floor and bending over throughout his bath. You can also place no-slip strips on the bottom of the tub to help prevent falls. In any event, you shouldn't let your baby stand in the tub (once he's able to) without keeping one hand on him all the time.

SPECIAL CARE

Skin care

Bathing your baby with water and a mild, unscented soap and then rinsing the skin thoroughly is all the skin care he is likely to need. Some parents apply powders and lotions to make their babies smell good and to keep their skin from drying out or chafing. As a matter of fact, the best way to avoid dry skin is not to bathe your baby too often. Use these products sparingly and note the following cautions:

• **Baby powders and cornstarch.** Neither is necessary for your baby's skin, and there's even some evidence that cornstarch may be a breeding ground for some of the infections that cause diaper rash. If you do use these products, do so cautiously so you don't create a cloud of powder that the baby might breathe. (Avoid using zinc stearate powders, since they irritate the lungs.) Apply any powder or cornstarch lightly to avoid caking it on your baby's skin.

• **Baby lotions and oil.** Baby lotions or oils are not necessary either, but your baby may love it if you gently massage him with a little lotion or oil after his bath. (See next page.) Be cautious if you're using mineral oils, since they can cause a rash in some babies.

The navel

The stump of the umbilical cord, which remains temporarily attached to the navel, should be kept clean, dry, and free from diaper irritation. After each bath and diaper change, swab it with a sterile cotton ball or cotton-tipped swab dipped in rubbing alcohol. When you're putting diapers on your infant, fold the front edge *below* the healing navel so it doesn't rub against that area. You don't need to put a sterile dressing on a navel that's healing normally.

The stump will fall off usually between ten and fourteen days after your baby's birth. Even after it has fallen off, continue to clean the navel with alcohol. Keep it dry, and watch it carefully until it completely heals over. After the stump has fallen off, there may be a little secretion or pinkish discharge from the navel. This is normal. However, any bloody discharge that continues for more than a week or any profuse bleeding should be reported to your physician. Any red swelling around a healing navel is also cause to call your physician.

The penis

Circumcised. Until the circumcised penis is healed (within about ten days of the operation), treat the tip with petroleum jelly after each diaper change and after a bath. The jelly will protect it against diaper irritation and encourage healing.

While the penis is healing, it is not uncommon for the wound to secrete a few drops of blood. This is normal and no cause for alarm. It is also normal for a healing penis to get a whitish coating on the tip. Once the circumcised penis heals, the only care it needs is normal washing.

Uncircumcised. The uncircumcised penis requires no special care. Wash it with warm, soapy water just as you would any other part of his body. When your boy is very young, you'll find it impossible to retract his foreskin. As he gets older, however, you'll find that his foreskin is more easily retractable, although it may not retract completely until age four. You may wish to follow this procedure to clean it: *gently* retract the foreskin, briefly wipe the penis with a washcloth, and then draw the foreskin down again. Don't be too aggressive about this, since there's a potential danger of getting the foreskin stuck back, causing a painful swelling of the tip.

Baby massage

Babies are especially sensitive to touch, so your infant may find a light, gentle massage extremely soothing and comforting. You can consult Frederick Leboyer's *Loving Hands* (Knopf, 1976), which beautifully describes the complete technique, or you can improvise by rubbing a little lotion or oil into your baby's skin after his bath. (Warm up the oil by setting the bottle in his bath water.) Starting with his neck, *slowly*, *gently*, and *rhythmically* work your way down to his feet. Don't forget his arms and hands. Then turn him over and massage his shoulders, back, and buttocks. Finally, massage his face, starting with the forehead, then the eyebrows, cheeks, and mouth.

Trimming fingernails

When your baby is very young, keeping his fingernails short is important for his own protection. During his finger play, he could easily scratch his face if his nails are not short and smoothly cut. As your child grows older, trimmed nails are for *your* protection. He'll delight in exploring your face with his hands, and long or ragged nails could unintentionally scratch you. At all times, short fingernails are a sensible hygienic measure for your baby. Dirt collects under his nails, and it'll be years before he quits putting his fingers in his mouth.

Here's what to do when you cut your baby's nails:

• Be sure to use a blunt-tipped fingernail scissors. Even the most docile, sleepy infant can make a sudden move that may cause you to poke him if you're using pointed scissors.

• Trim the fingernails (or toenails) when your baby is asleep or after a bath, when his nails are softer and easier to cut.

• Cut fingernails and toenails straight across, making sure you leave no ragged edges.

PUTTING YOUR BABY TO SLEEP

Sleep—your own and your baby's—will probably be on your mind frequently throughout your child's first year of life. As new parents, you'll find yourselves talking with anyone who will listen about how long (or how little) and how often (or how seldom) your baby sleeps. It can't be helped. Getting by on less sleep each night is one of the biggest adjustments you have to make as a new parent (mother or father), and although your chances of getting an uninterrupted night's rest increase as your baby gets older, it may be a few years before your sleep-life is back to what it was before you had a child.

As in many other things, babies vary in their sleep needs and habits. Your newborn may sleep for 22 hours a day, or he may get by on 12. If he's healthy, he's probably getting enough sleep, even if it seems "too much" or "too little" to you. You may be somewhat surprised by the nature of his sleep at this stage. Three kinds of sleep seem to characterize this early period: *quiet* sleep (which seems deep and calm), *active* sleep (which is accompanied by sucking, grimacing, and rapid eye movements), and *drifting* sleep (where your baby drowsily floats in and out of sleep). It's probably impossible for new parents not to check on their newborn at night, but don't be too alarmed at the snuffling noises and sometimes fretful sounds he makes. They're normal.

As he gets older, your baby may settle into a pattern of taking one or two good naps during the day and then sleeping for a solid stretch of time at night. (How long a stretch is another issue. See "Sleeping through the night," p. 32.) By the end of his first year, he may even give up one of those naps. Happily, the older your baby gets, the more active he'll become during the day, especially when he starts crawling and then walking. The more energy he spends during the day, the easier it will be to put him to sleep at night.

Basic equipment	A newborn doesn't need a crib. You can start him out in a bassinet, a cradle, a lined basket, or even a padded drawer or sturdy cardboard box. Just make sure the sides are high enough to prevent him from rolling out. As he gets older and bigger, of course, you'll move him to a crib. (See pp. 68-69 for what to look for in a crib.) Whether he sleeps in a bassinet or a crib, you'll want to make sure that you do the following: • Use a firm, nonallergenic mattress. (An inner-spring mattress will hold its shape longer than foam.) • Put a waterproof cover on the mattress, and stretch a fitted sheet on top of that. • Line the sides of the bed with bumpers or soft, washable fabric. • Don't use a pillow, which *could* smother your baby.
Surroundings	• Although a very young baby can sleep anywhere, it's probably a good idea, especially at night, to begin a routine of putting your baby to sleep in his own room. That way you won't be distracted at night by his snuffling and restless periods, and he will gradually come to associate a particular place with sleep-time.

- Try to keep the temperature of your baby's room around 70°F. (21.1°C.) if you can. During the winter, though, if you're trying to conserve energy or cut your heating bills, you *can* turn your thermostat down at night so long as you take care to wrap your baby in a blanket. Also, make sure his crib is not positioned next to a cold window and is as close to the heating vent or radiator as safety permits.

- When necessary, use a humidifier or cold air vaporizer in winter and a fan in summer, but don't put them too close to the bed. (Be sure you regularly clean the vaporizer; if you don't, it can become contaminated with organisms that can spread through the air when the vaporizer is turned on.)

- You don't need to hush the entire house when your baby sleeps. He'll easily get used to the normal noise levels. But try to avoid abrupt *changes* in the noise level that could cause him to startle and awaken.

- Make sure there are shades or curtains in your baby's room that you can draw to cut out sunlight during daytime naps.

- In warm weather, you can let your baby take naps outside, but don't put him in direct sunlight. Protect him against flies and mosquitoes with netting over the bassinet or carriage.

Getting your baby to sleep

During his first year, your baby will probably always need a little help (or a lot of it) going to sleep at night. It's difficult for a new baby to learn to shut out all the outside stimuli that must be tuned out before sleep is possible. It's a rare baby who, after being put in his crib and kissed goodnight, will drift off to sleep without protest. You'll often need to help soothe and quiet him first. This is often best accomplished by nursing him or giving him his bottle, but you can also try a few other ways if he's not hungry:

- Swaddle or rock him till he falls asleep.

- Car rides, carriage rides, swings, and the rhythm of your walk as you hold him will often lull an excited baby to sleep.

- Use soft, rhythmical background noise to lull him to sleep. It needn't be music; the monotonous drone of a fan, vaporizer, or air conditioner will work. Or you might try playing a recorded heartbeat over and over. If you start doing this right after his birth, he might be soothingly reminded of his blissful prenatal state.

- Put your baby across your lap and give him a gentle back rub.

- Fresh air seems to make babies sleepy. Take him outside or put his bed near an open window, if it's not too cold.

Sleep positions

- Many newborns sleep best on their stomachs. Before the umbilical cord heals, however, you may prefer to put your baby on his side, though this is not necessary if there's no infection.

- After a feeding, it's probably best to lay your baby on his right side. This helps digestion because the stomach, which is on the left side, can empty more easily into the intestinal tract, which is on the right. Don't put him on his back, however. If he spits up, he's more likely to choke.

Mixing up days and nights

Some babies, who get their days and nights mixed up, end up sleeping more during the day than at night, and that usually results in a baby who's wide awake and ready to play at 4 a.m. Here are some things you can do to reverse this:

- Treat daytime naps differently from nightly bedtime routines. During the day, let your baby take his naps anywhere in the house, but at night, put him in his own room.

- Don't let your baby sleep more than four uninterrupted hours during the day.

- Stimulate the baby more when he's awake during the day by singing, talking, or massaging him. But at night, be quiet and businesslike during feedings.

Sleeping through the night

When (or even whether) your baby starts to sleep through the night during his first year is one of the issues that new parents are often passionately concerned about. As a new parent, you'll probably *hear* about babies who have slept through the night since they were three months—or even three weeks—old, and you'll wonder why your child is still getting up twice a night at six months. There's not much to be gained by these kinds of comparisons, except frustration, so don't let them worry you too much.

Actually, very few babies will *really* sleep through the night without waking up during their first year of life. In a recent study of night-waking in infants, less than 20 percent of a group of nine-month-olds slept without waking at least once between midnight and 5 a.m. Another survey seems to show that breastfed babies are more prone to wake up during the night than bottlefed babies are.

The vexing question that parents have to face is really rather simple: if I'm sure that my baby is neither hungry nor sick, what should I do when he wakes up at night? While the question is simple, the answers are not— even the experts disagree on the best way to handle night-waking.

Some parents cannot bear to hear their infants cry at night. They reason that a crying infant must have some need that could be satisfied, and that it's best for the child if the parent attends to him promptly and tries to soothe him back to sleep. That way both the parent and the infant get back to sleep as soon as possible. By the second half of your child's first year, however, you may be reinforcing this behavior in your child and creating the expectation that you will always come when he wakes up at night.

Other parents try letting their infants cry when they wake at night, hoping that the infants will cry themselves back to sleep. This can be difficult, because it may mean listening to your baby cry for 15 to 20 minutes each time he wakes, and the process may take a few nights. The important thing is that you do something you feel comfortable with. You'll probably need to talk with other parents and your physician before you decide how to handle this issue. Babies have different temperaments, and no single solution will work for everyone.

COMFORTING A CRYING BABY

All babies cry, of course, and one of your first challenges as a new parent will be to figure out why your baby is crying and to learn how you can comfort him. Most babies can be comforted most of the time by having one of their basic needs met—food, a changed diaper, sleep, entertainment. Also, most babies seem to go through a "fussy" period each day when nothing seems to work but letting them "cry it out." The section below offers some suggestions about how to comfort your child when he's crying.

CAUSES	COMFORTS
Hunger	Most of the time a baby who's crying is hungry, and the obvious solution is to feed him.
Gas in stomach	To burp your baby, use one of the techniques described on p. 57. Some babies need one burp for every three to five minutes of feeding time. Some babies are "delayed burpers"—they may go for a half-hour between the end of their feeding and their first burp. Just keep trying.
Need to suck	Most babies are born with an intense sucking reflex. Not only is this a source of nourishment, but it also soothes and comforts them. If you're nursing your child, the breast is the best possible source of sucking comfort, but if it's clear that he's not hungry, you can offer him a pacifier or help him find his thumb or fingers for sucking.
Wet diapers	Change your baby's diapers if they're wet or soiled. (The average newborn needs ten to twelve diaper changes per day.) Even if changing your infant's diapers doesn't seem to solve the problem of his fussiness, at least by changing him you haven't contributed to the potential problem of diaper rash.
Temperature extremes	If your baby is too warm or too cold, he will cry out of discomfort. Try to be sensitive to your baby's needs and be sure not to overdress him, leave him in drafts, or take him out into cold weather if he's not properly bundled. A good rule of thumb is to keep your baby covered with the same amount of clothing you would need to keep yourself warm or to stay cool.
Boredom	Your baby can become bored, just as you can, and his cry can be a way of requesting some stimuli. You can do lots of things to entertain a bored baby (see pp. 81-85).
Loneliness	Babies need a great deal of physical contact, and it is impossible to give them too much. Remember that there's nothing "wrong" or "spoiled" about a baby who likes to be constantly held. (Everyone needs a good cuddle from time to time.) Try to arrange your schedule so you can give him a lot of contact.
Colic	If nothing seems to comfort your baby, and he's less than three or four months old, it's possible that he has colic. See p. 101 for more details and suggestions.

THUMBSUCKING AND PACIFIERS

Thumbsucking

All babies have a need to suck, and yours may need more sucking than breastfeeding or his bottle allow. Some babies suck their thumbs and fingers even before they're born. They seem to have a natural knack for comforting themselves in this way. If your baby hasn't found his own thumb, and you don't want to introduce a pacifier, you can help him find his thumb by gently guiding it into his mouth. This might help quiet and comfort him when he's fussy.

According to the American Dental Association, there is little reason to fear that thumb- or finger-sucking will harm a baby's teeth or jaws. In fact, it shouldn't be a matter of concern unless the child is three or four years old and sucking with a great deal of pressure on the jaws. As it happens, most babies give up the habit of thumbsucking when they're between eighteen months and two years of age. The practice may crop up infrequently after that point, especially in times of fatigue, stress, or fear, but this is natural and shouldn't be discouraged.

Pacifiers

A baby who has a great need to suck or who is difficult to comfort may find great comfort in a pacifier. The new orthodontic pacifiers on the market are designed not to interfere with the development of your child's teeth and jaws, and it's easier to wean a child from a pacifier than from a thumb (although removing a pacifier doesn't always mean a child won't suck his thumb).

Here's some helpful advice about using a pacifier:

• Be careful not to pop the pacifier into your baby's mouth whenever he seems fussy—make sure all of his basic needs (for food, dry clothes, warmth, cuddling) are satisfied first.

• If you let your baby have a pacifier in bed, he may begin to need it to fall asleep at night, and then wake up crying for it whenever it falls out of his mouth (which could happen several times a night). To eliminate this problem, try to remove the pacifier once your child gets sleepy.

• Never tie a pacifier around your child's neck. The string or cord could accidently strangle him.

• Never coat a pacifier with honey, since there's a possible connection between honey and infant botulism in the first year of life.

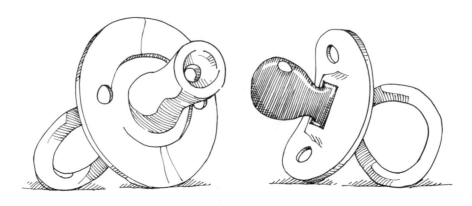

CLOTHING AND SHOES FOR YOUR BABY

Buying clothing

- Babies grow quickly during their first year of life, so don't be surprised if your infant rapidly outgrows his clothes. The average baby will double his birth weight in five to six months and triple it by the end of the year. Babies also generally grow eight inches (20 cm.) during their first year.

- Some clothing comes in a "newborn" or "three-month" size, but it may be more economical for you to buy a "six-month" or "up to 18 pounds" size and allow your baby to grow into it. Check the labels for weight as well as age; you may have a child who is smaller or larger than average. The following chart can be used as a general guide for determining your baby's size:

Weight	Size
Birth-13 lbs.	3 mos.
14-18 lbs.	6 mos.
19-22 lbs.	12 mos.
23-25 lbs.	18 mos.
26-28 lbs.	24 mos.
29-32 lbs.	36 mos.

- Many babies hate having clothes pulled over their heads. Look for shirts with side or front openings, shoulder snaps, or large, easily stretchable necklines. Buy clothing that also allows easy access to your baby's diapers for changing. That means open fronts, snap crotch and legs, or pants that can be removed easily.

- Look at how clothing is made. Most baby clothes will need numerous washings. Check for well-constructed seams and sturdy zippers. Are the seams soft inside? A scratchy seam can be very irritating to a baby's sensitive skin.

Dressing your baby

- Babies are able to produce heat from the time they are born. New babies, however, can't conserve the heat they make—they lose it as fast as they make it. As the baby grows, he gains more ability to conserve his own warmth and will need to expend less energy to keep warm. Here are some tips on dressing your child:

- In *warm weather*, babies are more often overdressed than underdressed. Overdressing causes rashes and excess sweating. In very warm temperatures, your baby should wear as little clothing as possible. If he seems uncomfortable, remove his plastic pants.

- In *cold weather*, use layers of clothing so you'll be able to add or subtract clothing in response to the temperature inside or out. For a newborn baby, a short trip in cold weather is usually fine if he is dressed properly. But a longer trip, especially if the baby falls asleep, may cause chilling.

- The older and more active your baby gets, the more difficult it will be to keep him still while you dress him. Happily, you'll be getting more efficient at the process, but you'll probably need to rely on games and songs to keep him quiet. You might also try keeping a special toy handy to keep him diverted.

- *To put on a shirt*, gather the neck opening into a loop. Slip it first over the back of your baby's head, then forward, stretching the opening forward as you bring it down gently past his forehead and nose so you won't scratch his face.

- To *pull on sleeves*, put your left hand up the sleeve and grasp your baby's hand. With your other hand, pull the sleeve over his arms.

- To *take off a shirt*, take his arms out of the sleeves first, then stretch the neckline open. Raise the front part of the neck opening past the nose and forehead, then slip the shirt off toward the back of the baby's head.

- To *put on a blanket sleeper or stretch suit*, it's often easier to start by spreading the sleeper or suit out on the changing table or bed and then laying your baby on top of it. Slide his legs in first, his arms next, and then zip or snap it up.

Shoes and socks

- Babies do not need shoes until they walk outside. Bare feet are fine before a baby walks and when he starts walking inside. In fact, they have several advantages over shoes: an infant's arches are relatively flat at first, so by using his feet he builds the arches up and strengthens his ankles; muscles, not shoes, support his feet; and bare feet are often safer, since the baby can use his toes for balance.

- The newly standing baby wearing his first shoes may find it difficult to balance, so he may fall more often until he gets used to wearing shoes.

- For the indoor walker on uncarpeted floors, avoid socks or booties that don't have slip-resistant soles. Socks can be very slippery.

- Take your baby along when you buy him new shoes. It's important to get a good fit. Make sure that shoes are measured for width and length. Shoes (and boots) should be checked for size every three months.

- Make sure you consider socks when fitting new shoes. Try shoes on with the appropriate weight sock for the season. (Socks should also fit well. A sock that is too small can constrict your baby's toes.)

- Have your baby stand or walk in the shoe to see how it fits. There should be 1/2 inch (1.25 cm.) of space beyond the longest toe for growth.

- Baby shoes are expensive, but it's not necessary to buy the most expensive, sturdiest shoe. As long as the shoe fits well and your baby is comfortable wearing it, an inexpensive shoe will do just as nicely as an expensive leather one. Tennis shoes, for instance, are perfectly appropriate for babies. They're soft, flexible, and less expensive than leather shoes. Although it's rarely necessary, have a baby with special shoe needs examined by a physician.

CLOTHING CHECKLIST

Below is a list of some of the types of clothes you'll find useful during your child's first year, plus suggestions for a reasonable number to have on hand. These are only suggestions, of course; the actual number you'll need will depend on how often you do laundry, the season, your child's age, and other factors.

FOR A NEWBORN:

Item	Number	Comments
__ **Undershirts**	4-6	Undershirts provide extra warmth when worn under other clothing, and in the summer your baby will usually be happy wearing just an undershirt and diaper. Available in slip-on or side-snap styles.
__ **Gowns**	4	These long-sleeved garments with a snap neckline and an open, closed, or drawstring bottom are good for the first few months but awkward when your baby starts to creep or crawl.
__ **Stretch suits**	4	These one-piece suits have front snaps that run from neck to foot, making it easy to change him. The suits can be worn day or night. Stretch material is comfortable and allows room for growth.
__ **Blanket sleepers**	3-4	These come in two forms: in a bag that allows room for growth, or shaped like coveralls with built-in feet. They usually have a front zipper.
__ **Receiving blankets**	4-6	Soft, light blankets have many uses — for swaddling a newborn; as light cover; as surface cover for changing; rolled up as extra padding or crib guard in a cradle, bassinet, car seat, or infant seat.

Item	Number	Comments
__ **Blankets**	2	Knitted shawls or blankets, often made of orlon or acrylic, are warm and washable. They wrap easily and stay tucked around your baby.
__ **Sweaters**	1-2	Usually made of orlon or acrylic, sweaters are available in front- or back-opening styles. (Wool sweaters are scratchy and harder to wash, and some babies are allergic to wool.)
__ **Booties/socks**	1-3 pr.	These are desirable or necessary only to keep your baby's feet warm in cooler outdoor temperatures, or in a cool house. Infant feet are naturally cool so let the temperature in house or outside be your guide.

FOR AN OLDER BABY

Item	Number	Comments
__ **Coveralls or overalls**	2-3	Coveralls and overalls are practical and comfortable for older babies who are starting to creep or crawl. The crawling baby needs extra padding for more active play, especially in knee and bottom areas. Most coveralls for young babies have snap crotch and legs for easy changing.
__ **Shirts**	2-3	Shirts (long- and short-sleeved) come in a variety of styles with crew necks and turtle necks, or with snaps or buttons down the front or on the shoulder. Make sure the shirt fits easily over your baby's head.
__ **Dresses**	—	Dresses are nice for older girls but not very practical for a small baby. They don't keep her legs warm and are often bothersome for the baby and parent, since they tend to bunch up. Choose shorter rather than longer styles — longer dresses tend to get in the crawling baby's way. In cooler weather, stretch tights should be worn under a dress.

FOR GOING OUTSIDE

Item	Number	Comments
__ **Hat**	1-2	Cotton or synthetic caps are good in the summer to protect your baby's head and face from direct sunlight. Knitted hats, usually made of orlon or wool, are useful in cooler weather when it's advisable to cover his head and ears.
__ **Snowsuit**	1	Snowsuits are made of heavy and durable material. Many have optional snap-on mittens and hoods. Choose a suit that's a little too large, since it will have to go over clothing. Avoid very slippery fabric — it's hard enough to hold a wiggly baby.
__ **Bunting**	1	This is a bag made of soft, heavy fabric — often quilted or lined — and it is usually made with a front zipper. It's good for outings in cooler weather, and it allows your baby room to move and grow. Not an essential item.
__ **Pram suit**	1	Pram suits enclose a baby's legs and feet separately. They may come in one or two pieces, which zip or snap from neck to foot, and they're usually made of quilted fabric, acrylic, or wool. Not an essential item. (A warm shawl wrapped around your baby may do just as well.)

Chapter 3

FEEDING YOUR BABY

Some of the deepest joys of early parenthood are in store for you when you feed your baby. Nothing can compete for beauty with the picture of your blissful, weeks-old infant contentedly sucking at the breast or bottle and gradually easing off to sleep. There is no more cherished sensation than the feeling of your own child, nestled warm and relaxed in your arms, receiving from you the nourishment that she vitally needs.

How to provide this nourishment is the subject of this chapter. A baby will grow more during her first year than at any other time in her life. Her weight will generally triple by her first birthday, and she'll typically grow eight inches (20 cm.). (See the weight and length charts on pp. 131-132.) What she takes in nutritionally has a great deal to do with how well she grows.

Not surprisingly, then, most parents give serious thought to the question of how they're going to feed their newborn—with breast milk or formula. It's not a decision you can put off making: you'll need to decide before your baby is born. Each option requires some preparation and special equipment.

The American Academy of Pediatrics recommends that mothers breastfeed their infants, since no formula can rival breast milk, which is perfectly compatible with a baby's needs. Nor can a plastic bottle exactly imitate the sensation of the breast. But there are advantages to both methods of feeding (see p. 42), so you'll need to look closely at your own special circumstances in order to decide. Remember: happy, healthy, and well-adjusted babies have been brought up on each method.

When your infant is about six months old, she'll be ready to start eating solids, and your concern over her getting a balanced diet will increase. Once she starts making her personal likes and dislikes known, as she will when she has the opportunity to choose between apples and peas—or nothing at all— your control starts to diminish. Your baby's own personal style also emerges—she may be an easygoing eater, a vigorous masher, an energetic thrower, or a combination of all types, depending on the time of day, her mood, or who knows what!

But eating solid foods also presents a major milestone in your baby's first year. She's clearly on the road to independence—to no longer being a baby.

BREASTFEEDING AND BOTTLEFEEDING

Advantages of Breastfeeding

• Breast milk is nature's milk, and it can't be perfectly duplicated in formulas. The composition of breast milk is ideally suited to the nutritional needs of a newborn.

• Before the actual milk comes in, a mother's breasts produce *colostrum*, a yellowish, watery fluid that contains important antibodies and the proper nourishment for a newborn baby.

• Breastfeeding provides immunities that help keep the breastfed infant from getting sick. Breastfed babies are also troubled with fewer allergies.

• You're less likely to overfeed a breastfed baby, who will just stop nursing when she's full. There's no need to worry about your baby gaining too much weight.

• Breastfeeding your child is convenient, economical, and time-saving. You don't have to bother with bottles and formula. Traveling with a breastfed baby is simple, since you don't have bags of equipment to carry around.

• The stools of a breastfed infant are mild smelling and inoffensive to clean up, and breastfed babies are less likely to have diarrhea.

• Breastfeeding is a pleasant way to provide the warm, human contact that is so important in early infant development, and it's a very good way to satisfy the strong sucking urge that babies have.

• Because making breast milk uses up calories in the mother, and because breastfeeding causes the uterus to quickly contract to its prepregnancy size, a nursing mother will generally regain her figure faster than a mother who's bottlefeeding her child.

Advantages of Bottlefeeding

• The mother of a bottlefed baby is not the child's sole source of sustenance. Other people can easily feed the child if she decides to go back to work or out for an afternoon.

• When an infant is bottlefed, her father can actively take part in feedings and take equal responsibility for the nighttime feedings, thus letting a postpartum mother get a few extra hours of much-needed sleep.

• The mother of a bottlefed baby doesn't have to worry about how her breast milk will be affected by what she eats or drinks, what medications she takes, and how much rest she gets.

• Parents of a bottlefed baby know exactly how much milk their baby is getting and can control how much she's offered.

• With bottlefeeding, there is no risk of embarrassment involved in feeding the baby in public.

BREASTFEEDING BASICS

Preparations

If you plan to breastfeed your child, it's best to prepare your nipples during the last trimester of your pregnancy so that you can reduce the likelihood of sore nipples later on. Here are some things you can do:

- Wash your nipples with water only, not with soap, which can remove the natural protection of the skin's own oils.

- Toughen your nipples by rubbing them briskly with a towel after bathing. You can also toughen nipples by rubbing lanolin or topical vitamin lotions on them after they've air dried.

- Massage your breasts. With the palm of your hand, press down and inward under the arm and below the collarbone, moving your palm in a circular motion. Press around the nipple with the thumb and knuckle of your first finger, and then move the pressure out to the end of the nipple. You may express a few drops of liquid.

- If your nipples are inverted, you can still breastfeed a baby. Discuss this with your physician, because there are several steps you can take during your third trimester to prepare your nipples.

Size of breasts

The size of your breasts has absolutely nothing to do with your ability to nurse. Milk is produced in glands deep within the chest and is in no way influenced by the amount of surface fat that makes up the visible breast.

"Let-down" reflex

Generally, milk doesn't flow from the breast the second the baby begins to suck. It often takes a few minutes for the sucking to trigger what is known as the "let-down" reflex. Stimulation on the baby's part and relaxation on the mother's trigger a release of hormones from the pituitary glands. These hormones in turn cause the milk to be "let down" from the awaiting milk glands and ducts.

Many mothers experience this reflex as a not unpleasant tingling "pins-and-needles" feeling around the tip of the breast, a feeling that fades as the nursing session progresses. It's a phenomenon that frequently disappears altogether after a mother has been breastfeeding her child for a number of months. Whether or not you feel the tingling of the let-down, you'll know it's happening by listening to your baby's regular and satisfied gulps as she easily draws the milk out of your breasts. If you have trouble getting let-down, some physicians recommend an artificial hormone, which can be sprayed in the nose, that helps release the milk in the breasts.

Supply and demand

The more your baby sucks and the more frequently she empties your breasts, the more milk you will make, because your milk production works on a "supply-and-demand" system. It's especially important during those first weeks of your child's life to let her nurse as often as she desires so that you can build up an adequate milk supply. Too frequent exposure to an artificial nipple when you're just establishing your milk supply can potentially interfere with your baby's successful attachment to your breast. (See "Supplemental feedings," p. 44.) And if your baby is full of supplemental formula, she won't suck at your breasts, which will then be deprived of the signals they need to produce as much milk as your baby needs. If your baby seems hungry fairly soon after a nursing session, you should put her to the breast again. It won't be long before your breasts are producing enough milk to keep her full for a few hours.

Scheduling

- Breastfed babies should be nursed on demand—that is, according to their own time schedule.

- A newborn will need to nurse frequently—sometimes as many as a dozen or more times a day. It is important to let her nurse often because a mother's breasts need the frequent stimulation that the sucking will give them to build up milk production.

- Some breastfed babies fall into a fairly predictable feeding schedule after two or three weeks. A common one is nursing every two to four hours, often with a longer stretch of sleep at night. But not all babies readily establish a regular schedule, and those who do sometimes change schedules periodically. Every baby is different and the right schedule is the one that keeps her happy.

- Even if your breastfed baby has been nursing on a fairly regular schedule for a few weeks, it's very normal for her to suddenly break that schedule and need to nurse more frequently. A growth spurt may be signaling her to suck more frequently and thus encourage your breast to meet her increasing needs. Growth spurts typically take place at six weeks, three months, and six months of life.

Colostrum

What a nursing baby will receive during her first nursing sessions, before the actual milk comes in, is called colostrum. This watery, yellowish substance is high in nourishing proteins and full of immunities that protect babies from harmful infections. Your baby's need for colostrum makes early and frequent feeding sessions very important.

First milk

Milk commonly "comes in" from two to six days after birth—on the late side if this is the mother's first child, and on the early side if she has given birth before.

Which breast first?

Your baby will suck most vigorously at the first breast you offer her in a nursing session, since she's most hungry when she sucks from this breast. Because this vigorous sucking is the best signal your breast can receive to produce more milk, you'll want to make sure that both breasts are receiving equal signals. So alternate which breast you offer first at each nursing.

Supplemental feedings

During the first few weeks, you should devote yourself exclusively to getting your nursing baby onto the breast. After that, however, an artificial nipple (preferably an "orthodontic" one) can be introduced. If it's offered once or twice a week with either expressed breast milk or formula, it won't interfere with milk production, and it will allow your baby to feed well from either the breast or the bottle.

Engorgement

When the milk first comes in, your breasts will frequently feel temporarily engorged. Even though this feeling subsides within a few days, it can be an uncomfortable, painful experience. To ease the discomfort, take hot baths and put washcloths as hot as you can stand on each breast; then express some of the milk. And by all means, let your baby nurse as much as she wants to. Later, you may also feel engorged when your baby goes too long between feedings. The same treatments will work then.

How long to nurse

Sore nipples are common among breastfeeding mothers, even those with their second or third breastfed child. The soreness can last several days, and it may linger temporarily. To avoid soreness, or to keep it at a minimum, you may want to increase the length of each nursing session gradually, until your nipples have become conditioned. Try this schedule for each session:

First day	Five minutes on each breast
Second day	Seven minutes on each breast
Third and fourth day	Ten minutes on each breast
Fifth day	As long as she wants — but usually not more than ten to fifteen minutes on each breast

Keep in mind that you'll need to modify this suggested schedule, depending on how rapidly your milk "lets down." (See p. 43.) Generally, a nursing infant will get 90 percent of her milk in the first five minutes of any given nursing session. But if it takes five minutes of sucking before your baby is receiving any significant amount of milk you'll need to lengthen each of the above times so that you're not ending a nursing session just as it actually gets started.

Vitamin supplements

Before a breastfed baby starts to eat solid foods, many pediatricians will recommend that the parents supplement feedings with fluoride and vitamin D, just in case the mother's breast milk does not meet the recommended daily allowances.

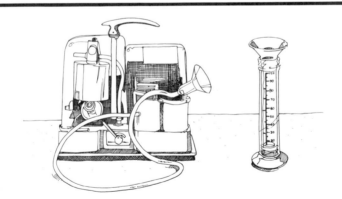

Expressing milk

A variety of excellent breast pumps are available that allow you to express milk for later use, giving you the opportunity, if you wish, to work outside the home *and* provide breast milk for your baby. Expressing milk, of course, also keeps your milk production up. The graduated cylinder pumps and the electric pumps (which can sometimes be rented) are very effective—much more effective than expressing milk by hand.

Milk that's been expressed can be stored in plastic containers in the freezer. After the expressed milk has cooled, it can be added onto previously frozen layers and saved for months. Once a batch of frozen breast milk has been thawed, however, it should be kept in the refrigerator and used within three days. It should not be refrozen.

Care of breasts

- You'll probably want to wear a nursing bra while you're breastfeeding your child for the convenience it offers. You'll especially want to make sure that any bra you wear while nursing is well fitted. A bra that presses or binds can be more than uncomfortable—it can cause clogged milk ducts or even a breast infection.

- Make sure your nipples are dry after each feeding. Leave them exposed to the air for 15 minutes if possible.

- Carefully wash your breasts at least twice a day to remove any traces of milk. But don't use soap when you wash them—it removes the natural oils and can lead to cracked nipples.

- If you're bothered by leaking nipples, you can keep your clothes dry by lining your bra with disposable cotton squares or breast pads. Don't use waterproof liners and try to avoid bras that aren't cotton—they don't let the air in.

- If your nipples are inverted, they'll probably need special attention. Discuss this with your physician. It may be helpful to wear Swedish milk cups between feedings.

Mastitis

Mastitis is a breast infection that can occur as a result of a clogged milk duct. The breast will become reddened and tender. The infection can cause a fever and make you ache and feel nauseated. The recommended treatment is to apply heat to the sore area for ten minutes every six hours and to *increase* the frequency of nursing from the affected breast. You should also contact your physician, who may want to prescribe antibiotics to clear up the infection.

Biting

Once a breastfed baby gets upper and lower teeth, she may start biting your nipples while she's nursing. It's important to remember that this biting is in no way malicious, nor does it suggest that your child wants to be weaned. Her gums may still be bothering her from her new teeth or from teeth that are yet to break through, and it simply feels good for her to bite on anything she can get her mouth around.

No one is going to pretend that biting doesn't hurt or that it should be ignored. It typically happens, though, at the end of a nursing session when a child has had enough to eat and is simply playing around. So gently, but firmly, say "no" to your child as soon as you feel her bite down, and remove her from the breast. When this approach is used consistently, most babies learn not to bite.

WHAT A NURSING MOTHER NEEDS

Diet	While you're nursing, be sure to eat well-balanced, nutritious meals high in calcium and protein (see diet below). Your milk can contain only the vitamins and minerals you provide for it, and your body needs help to recover from the delivery of your child. Your physician may recommend a vitamin supplement. Although many nursing mothers have found these helpful in avoiding deficiencies, they're no substitute for nutritious food.
Liquids	Nursing mothers need to drink plenty of liquids (eight to ten glasses a day) to insure an adequate milk supply. It's a good idea to get into the habit of drinking a glass of water or unsweetened fruit juice before and after each nursing session.
Rest	Adequate rest is essential to a good milk supply, especially during those early postpartum weeks when you're still recovering. Get some extra sleep when your baby naps, and try to ignore all of those things you'd like to get done.
Relaxation	Work at being relaxed and unruffled, especially just before you nurse your baby. Emotional tensions can interfere with your let-down reflex and can keep your baby from getting the milk she needs.

A NURSING MOTHER'S DIET

A nursing mother needs about 2,500 calories a day (200 to 500 more than you needed when you were pregnant). Work at getting the appropriate number of servings from each of the four food groups. Each of the examples represents either one or a portion of one serving.

Food group	Servings per day	Examples
Vegetable-Fruit I vitamin A source (orange or green vegetables) and I vitamin C source (citrus fruit)	4	• ½ c. (125 ml.) cooked fruit • I whole medium fruit • ½ grapefruit • I dinner-size salad containing dark green, leafy vegetables
Bread-Cereal	4	• 2 slices of bread • ½-¾ c. (125-188 ml.) cooked cereal, pasta, rice • I oz. (28 gr.) ready-to-eat cereal
Milk-Cheese	4	• I c. (250 ml.) milk • I c. (250 ml.) yogurt • I oz. (28 gr.) cheddar cheese (= ¾ serving) • ½ c. (125 ml.) cottage cheese (= ¼ serving)
Meat-Poultry-Fish-Beans	2	• 2-3 oz. (56-84 gr.) lean meat, fish, poultry • I egg (= ½ serving) • ½-¾ c. (125-188 gr.) cooked dry beans (= ½ serving) • 2 Tbsp. (30 ml.) peanut butter (= ½ serving)

PUTTING YOUR BABY TO THE BREAST

WHAT TO DO

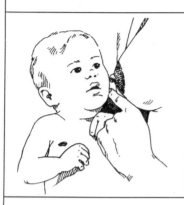

1 First evoke your infant's rooting reflex (see p. 12) by stroking the cheek nearest to the breast you want her to nurse from.

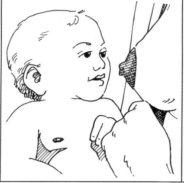

2 Her reflex action will be to turn toward the breast with a ready mouth. Once your baby becomes a more experienced nurser, she'll want to suck as soon as she feels the pressure of your bare breast on her cheek.

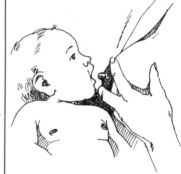

3 Help your baby find the nipple by placing your middle finger and forefinger in a scissors-like fashion on either side of the areola (the dark area around the nipple). Then, as you guide the nipple into her mouth, gently press downward with your top finger. This will cause the nipple to turn up slightly and make it more accessible to your baby's searching mouth.

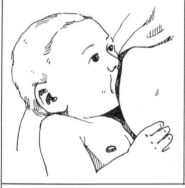

4 As she finds the nipple, she'll close her mouth around it and begin sucking. To insure proper sucking, make sure your baby takes a good deal of the areola in her mouth along with the nipple (how much will depend on the size of both your areola and your baby's mouth) and make sure her tongue is down.

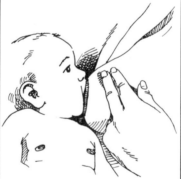

5 Be sure your baby's nose isn't completely buried in your breast as she nurses. If her nose is blocked, she can't breathe out of her mouth and nurse at the same time. Either change your position slightly so her nostrils are free, or gently use your finger to depress your breast above the areola to give her a breathing space.

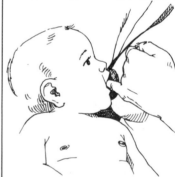

6 To end a nursing session, gently insert your little finger into the corner of your baby's mouth, between your areola and her gums. This will break the suction hold of your baby's mouth on your nipple. Pulling your nipple out of the baby's mouth causes undue strain on it and can make it sore. Proceed to burp your baby. (See p. 57.)

NURSING POSITIONS

Lying down

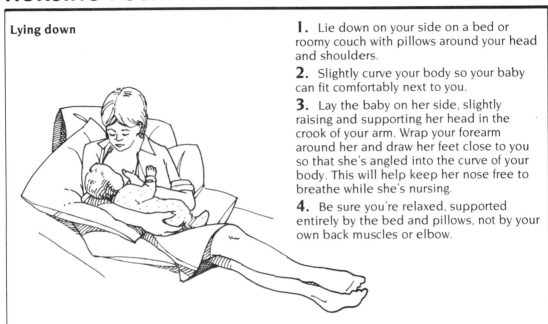

1. Lie down on your side on a bed or roomy couch with pillows around your head and shoulders.

2. Slightly curve your body so your baby can fit comfortably next to you.

3. Lay the baby on her side, slightly raising and supporting her head in the crook of your arm. Wrap your forearm around her and draw her feet close to you so that she's angled into the curve of your body. This will help keep her nose free to breathe while she's nursing.

4. Be sure you're relaxed, supported entirely by the bed and pillows, not by your own back muscles or elbow.

Sitting

1. Be sure to use a comfortable, well-padded easy chair or rocker. You may want to put a pillow behind your back for support or under your baby to bring her into a more convenient nursing position.

2. Avoid bending over while nursing — it will make you tense and you'll end up with a backache.

3. Support your baby with the cradle hold or in the "football" position (see p. 16), making sure her head is well-supported and she's sitting at a slight angle, with her head higher than her stomach. (This makes air bubbles burp up more easily.)

4. Face the baby toward you, making sure her head is close to your breast, but is tilted back slightly so her nose is free to breathe.

WEANING FROM THE BREAST

When?
There is no "right time" for weaning a baby. Some authorities suggest four months; others, two years. Only you can decide what will work best for you and your child. Many children will wean themselves when they're ready. This is often the least traumatic and most conflict-free way to wean, if you have the leisure. If the weaning is more your choice than your child's, she may need additional attention, especially if she has nursed a long time. Try to give her all the extra cuddling and care you can.

How?
How you wean is more important than when you wean. Be sure to do it gradually, gently, and with plenty of love and patience.

• Be as flexible as you can with the weaning. If it's at all possible, don't establish strict goals or rigid schedules.

• You'll want to avoid sudden weaning for two reasons: sudden weaning can cause a dramatic decline in the mother's hormonal flow and may trigger depression that's compounded by the abrupt loss of the special, close nursing relationship. Sudden weaning can also be traumatic for the child who has learned to gain comfort and solace (as well as nourishment) from the breast.

• When you wean, gradually cut back one feeding at a time—the lunchtime feeding is usually the first to go. Offer your baby her milk or juice from a cup along with her regular meal.

• If you're weaning from the breast to formula or cow's milk and your baby doesn't seem to like the taste, try a mixture of half breast milk and half formula or cow's milk.

• Many babies cling the longest to the nighttime feeding, others to the morning.

• A baby weaned early may miss sucking, especially at bedtime, in which case you may want to introduce a bottle or a pacifier.

• Breastfed babies, unless they're very young, often don't need to transfer from breast to bottle. They can be weaned directly to a cup. A weighted, two-handled cup with a spout is ideal for the inexperienced drinker.

• If you're weaning gradually, you shouldn't suffer the discomfort of engorged breasts. But if you do happen to become uncomfortable because of a missed feeding, express some milk from your breasts—just until you're fairly comfortable again. Don't express too much, though, or you'll stimulate milk production.

• If your child is progressing well with her weaning and suddenly suffers from teething or a cold, don't be surprised if she shows an increased need to nurse. You'll certainly not want to deny her the comfort of the breast while she's miserable; when she starts to feel better, she'll soon be able to resume weaning where she left off.

BOTTLEFEEDING BASICS

Y ou can feed a baby either formula or expressed breast milk from a bottle. An earlier section on breastfeeding discussed expressing milk for later use. Although this section will concentrate on bottlefeeding using infant formula, you can also follow the procedures on p. 55 if you're giving expressed breast milk to your baby.

Kinds of formula	Infant formulas contain the major nutrients that babies need. Since vitamins are added to formulas, no vitamin supplement is necessary, and if either powdered or liquid concentrate forms are used, your baby will get all the fluoride she needs from the water supply. (If your water is not fluoridated, a supplement may be prescribed.)
	Regarding the kind of formula you give your baby, the American Academy of Pediatrics recommends that you use iron-fortified formulas for the first year. If formula without iron is prescribed, another source of iron may be recommended. You *may* worry that your baby will become constipated on formula with iron, because some mothers become constipated while taking iron during their pregnancy. Actually, iron can cause either diarrhea or constipation, but usually causes neither. Continue giving your baby either iron-fortified formula or an iron supplement; if constipation becomes a problem, it can be handled in other ways.
	Infant formulas are available in three forms—powdered, liquid concentrate, and ready-to-use.
	• **Powdered** formulas can be mixed with tap water, are light to carry and easy to store, are the least expensive of formulas, and are available in 14- to 16-ounce (400- to 454-gr.) cans and single-feeding packets.
	• **Liquid concentrates** can be mixed with tap water, are easy to prepare, and are available in 13-fluid-ounce (384-ml.) cans. One can of concentrate may be refrigerated for up to 48 hours after opening, but then must be thrown away if it is not used.
	• **Ready-to-use** formulas can be poured directly into bottles and used without any mixing. Ready-to-use formulas are more expensive than powdered or liquid concentrate formulas. They are available in 8- or 32- fluid-ounce (256- or 946-ml.) cans and 4- and 8-fluid-ounce (128- or 256- ml.) bottles.
Storing formula	• After you've opened a container of *liquid* or *ready-to-use* formula and prepared a batch of bottles, you should cover and store the remaining formula in the refrigerator. It should be used within 48 hours.
	• Once you've opened a can of *powdered* formula, you should cover the can and store it in a cool, dry place. The can will indicate how long you can use the formula.
	• Once you've prepared a bottle of formula, either use it immediately or refrigerate it. You can safely use refrigerated bottled formula for 48 hours after preparation.
	• You can leave a bottle at room temperature for up to an hour without worrying about bacterial build-up in the formula (a half-hour in hot weather). If your baby has taken part of it, be sure to throw it away after an hour. But if she hasn't touched it, you can safely put it back in the refrigerator and use it later.

Equipment you need

The equipment you need to bottlefeed your baby depends in part on what kind of formula you use. The basic equipment required is listed below.

• eight to ten 8-ounce (or 240-ml.) **bottles**. (Both glass and plastic bottles are available. You can also use disposable bottles, which are plastic, sterilized sacks that you can buy in a roll, tear off, use once in a special holder, and then throw away.)

• eight to ten **caps or covers**

• eight to ten **screw-on rings**

• eight to ten **nipples**

• a **bottle brush**

• a **nipple brush**

• a **measuring pitcher** that is graduated in ounces (or ml.); one with a cover is especially handy

• a **funnel**

• a large, long-handled **spoon**

Care for equipment

• Thoroughly rinse the formula from each bottle immediately after it's used.

• Separately wash each bottle, ring, and nipple in hot, soapy water, using the bottle and nipple brushes. Carefully squeeze water through the nipples to make sure you remove all milk residue. Or wash everything in the dishwasher.

• Rinse everything in hot, clean water and let air dry.

PREPARING FORMULA

WHAT YOU NEED TO KNOW

• As long as you follow the instructions for cleaning the feeding equipment you use (see previous page) and are careful to wash your hands in hot, soapy water before you prepare a batch of formula, there's no need to sterilize any of the equipment or the water you use. Common sense and good personal hygiene are sufficient.

• Be sure to mix the formula exactly as your physician prescribes or as the formula manufacturer recommends.

• Prepare *powdered* or *liquid concentrates* using the procedures described below. *Ready-to-use* formulas need no preparation; you simply pour them into clean bottles.

WHAT TO DO

1 Wash your hands thoroughly with soap and hot water. If you're opening a can of concentrated formula, clean the top of the can.

2 Fill a clean measuring pitcher or a bottle with the amount of water you'll need. If you'll be adding powdered formula, use warm water to help it dissolve properly.

3a **Powdered formula.** Add the powdered formula using the scoop provided. Generally you mix a level scoop of powdered formula with every 2 ounces (60 ml.) of water. Stir or shake well.

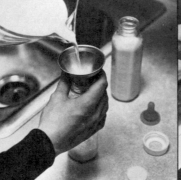

3b **Liquid concentrates.** Pour in the concentrated formula. Generally, concentrated formula is mixed with an equal amount of water. Stir well.

4 Pour the formula into clean bottles if you're preparing a whole batch. (A funnel makes the job easier.)

5 Put the nipples (inverted), caps, and rings on the bottles. Store the bottles in the refrigerator. (See "Storing formula," p. 51.)

HOW TO BOTTLEFEED

How much?

• Try to stay a bit ahead of your baby in how much formula you offer. Begin by offering 3 ounces (90 ml.) at each feeding, and as soon as she starts emptying the bottle at two or three feedings each day, start adding ½ ounces (15 ml.) of formula to each bottle. With time, she will work herself up to eight ounces (240 ml.) a feeding. Generally, you can follow the rough guidelines below for the first year. But remember to let her decide how much she wants.

AGE	AMOUNT PER DAY
Birth to 1 month	18-24 oz. (540-720 ml.)
1 to 2 months	22-26 oz. (660-780 ml.)
2 to 3 months	24-26 oz. (720-780 ml.)
3 to 4 months	24-28 oz. (720-840 ml.)
4 to 5 months	24-30 oz. (720-900 ml.)
5 to 6 months	24-32 oz. (720-960 ml.)
6 months to 1 year	24-32 oz. (720-960 ml.)

• Don't worry if your baby doesn't take much formula at any given feeding. Just as your appetite fluctuates, so does hers. If she's happy and thriving in every other way, but barely touches a bottle periodically, it's nothing to worry about.

• Sometimes a baby will stop sucking in the middle of a feeding. Don't mistake this for lack of interest—she's probably just resting. Be patient, and when she's ready she'll start eating again. But don't force a bottle if it's clear she doesn't want any more, and don't nudge every last drop of formula into your infant if it's clear she's not interested.

Scheduling and demand

• Bottlefed babies will usually go from two to four hours between feedings, and will eventually go for a longer stretch at night.

• Imposing a strict feeding schedule on a very young bottlefed baby is not a good idea, since it may result in more anxiety for the mother or father and more discomfort for the newborn than are necessary. Offering a bottle to a baby whenever she seems hungry will not spoil her. Just make sure her needs do not lie elsewhere (a change of diaper; a quieter, warmer room; a few close cuddles in a rocking chair). Her digestive system will soon adjust to a two- to four-hour schedule that you can count on, and even that will lengthen as she gets older.

• Don't wake your baby in the middle of the night for a feeding. If she's hungry, she'll wake herself.

GIVING THE BOTTLE TO YOUR BABY

WHAT YOU NEED TO KNOW

• Although formula at almost any temperature can be given to your baby, she may prefer it slightly warm. If you're making up a bottle of formula using tap water, simply draw water at the desired temperature. If you want to warm up a cold bottle, just set it in a pan of water on the stove for a few minutes or set the bottle in a pan in the sink and run hot water over it. (Be careful if you use a microwave oven to heat formula, since the formula can become very hot, while the bottle remains cool.) Test the formula on the inside of your wrist to make sure it's not too hot. Hot milk, of course, can scald a baby's tongue and mouth.

• Check the flow of milk from the nipple before each feeding. The milk should *drip* out steadily. If it comes out *too slowly*, your baby will tire of sucking before she's had her fill and probably swallow a lot of air in the process. You can enlarge a nipple hole with a hot needle. If the milk comes out *too quickly*, your baby will be full before she sucks as much as she needs to. And she may try to slow the stream of milk by thrusting her tongue up against the nipple. This "tongue

thrust" can be detrimental to the placement of her teeth and to later tooth development. Throw away the nipple if the milk flows too quickly.

• It's important that air get into the bottle and displace the formula—otherwise, the baby will not be able to suck anything out. So keep the bottle cap slightly loose to allow air to enter. You can tell that your baby is successfully feeding if you observe a constant stream of bubbles rising through the formula.

• Avoid propping a bottle or teaching your infant to hold it herself. If left alone with a bottle, an infant could choke on the formula. And, more importantly, every baby vitally needs cuddling and love to accompany a feeding.

• Avoid putting your baby to bed with a bottle. A baby who feeds lying down has a greater tendency to get an ear infection. And falling asleep with a bottle in her mouth can lead to tooth decay, even if your baby's teeth have not yet erupted.

WHAT TO DO

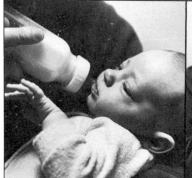

1 To introduce a bottle to your baby, hold her in your lap, circled in the crook of your arm, and gently touch her cheek nearest you with the nipple of the bottle. This will trigger her rooting reflex (see p. 12), and she'll turn toward you with an open mouth, searching for the nipple.

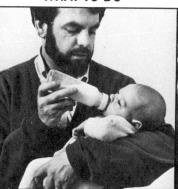

2 Be sure to hold your baby with her head and upper body raised at a slight angle while you feed her. It's easier for her to swallow the milk in this position than if she's lying flat on her back.

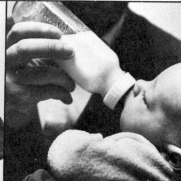

3 Try to keep the neck of the bottle constantly filled with milk by tipping it upward as you feed your baby. This helps keep her from swallowing too much air. When it's clear that your baby is finished, proceed to burp her (see p. 57).

WEANING FROM THE BOTTLE

When?
- There is no clear "right time" to wean a baby from the bottle, but it can be comfortably done as soon as the baby is old enough to get her milk from a cup. The process can begin when your child is anywhere from five months to one year old.

How?
- How you wean your baby is more important than *when* you do it. Be sure to wean her gradually, gently, with plenty of love and patience.
- Weaning from the bottle is often easily done by occasionally introducing liquids (especially formula or breast milk) out of a cup. A weighted, two-handled cup with a spout is ideal for the inexperienced drinker.
- If your child is strongly attached to the bottle and refuses to take milk from a cup, don't despair. Just continue offering it to her, keep your attitude casual, and when she does start taking a sip or two (which she eventually will), don't force more. She'll catch on at her own pace.
- Weaning will be easier if, once your child is mobile, you let her have a bottle only while you're holding her in your lap. You'll need to be firm, but her delight in her new-found motor skills will gradually supercede her interest in the bottle.
- When you wean gradually, cut back one feeding at a time—the lunchtime one is usually the first to go. Offer your baby her milk or juice from a cup, along with her regular meal.
- Many babies cling the longest to the night feeding, others to the morning.
- If you're progressing along well with weaning, and your child suddenly suffers from teething or a cold, don't be surprised if she shows an increased need for the bottle. You'll certainly not want to deny her that source of comfort while she's miserable; when she starts feeling better, she'll soon be able to pick up weaning where she left off.

BURPING YOUR BABY

WHAT YOU NEED TO KNOW

• When a baby takes a bottle or nurses, she often swallows air that can make her uncomfortable until she burps it up.

• Unless your baby is unusually fussy, one burp during a feeding and one burp after are usually enough.

• Try not to interrupt your baby's feeding to burp her. Take advantage of her pauses in sucking and use them as burp times. If you're breastfeeding, try to burp her before you switch her to your other breast.

• It is not always necessary to get a burp from your baby. If one does not come up in a few minutes, resume feeding her and try again later if she's fussy.

• Before you burp your baby, drape a diaper or towel across your shoulder or knees to catch any spitup.

• When you put your baby down after a feeding, be sure to place her on her stomach. That way she'll be able to more easily release any *additional* trapped air, and she won't choke on any milk or mucous she does spit up.

• Handle your baby gently after a feeding. Bouncing or jiggling her may cause her to spit up milk with a burp.

• Spitting up some milk with a burp is quite common among infants. If it isn't caused by too much swallowed air or too large a meal, it is often due to the immature muscles that control the passage between the stomach and the esophagus. In any case, the spitting up will decrease as your baby grows, so if she's thriving and content in every other way, it's nothing to worry about.

• If your baby seems to be spitting up unusually large amounts of milk, try holding her in a more upright position when you feed her, so that the air she swallows is not trapped below the milk in her stomach. It may also help to keep your baby at an upright angle for at least a half-hour to an hour after a feeding if she has a tendency to spit up.

• Spitting up in a bottlefed baby may be an indication that you're overfeeding her.

WHAT TO DO

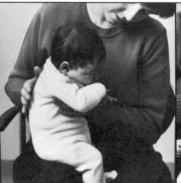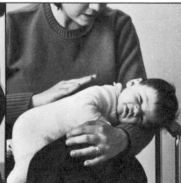

First method: Hold your baby upright with her head over your shoulder. Gently rub or pat her back until she burps.

Second method: Place your baby so she's sitting on your lap and leaning slightly forward. Be sure to support her head and back. Gently rub or pat her back until she burps.

Third method: Lay your baby face down across your lap or a mattress. Turn her head to one side and support it with one hand. Gently rub or pat her back until she burps.

INTRODUCING SOLID FOODS

When?

A baby is ready for solid foods when she's around six months old. By then, her digestive system is well-enough developed to handle solids, and she begins to need the additional calories and nutrients that solid foods offer. Your baby will let you know when she's ready for solids. Breast milk or formula won't completely satisfy her, or she'll show increased interest in more nursing sessions or formula feedings, an interest that won't subside in two or three days (as it will with a growth spurt). New teeth that make a baby eager to chew also suggest she's ready for more than breast milk or formula.

Why wait?

It is important not to introduce solids too soon for a number of reasons:

• For a very young baby, breast milk is the ideal, and formula the most nearly ideal, food the baby can have. Feeding an infant solids too soon only fills her up with inferior foods, and she could suffer nutritionally.

• Delaying the introduction of solid foods helps avoid food-induced allergies and allergic manifestations, like eczema and asthma.

• It is possible that introducing solid foods too early may contribute to obesity later on.

• Despite rumor, it has never been clearly demonstrated that giving cereal at bedtime during infancy will help a baby sleep through the night.

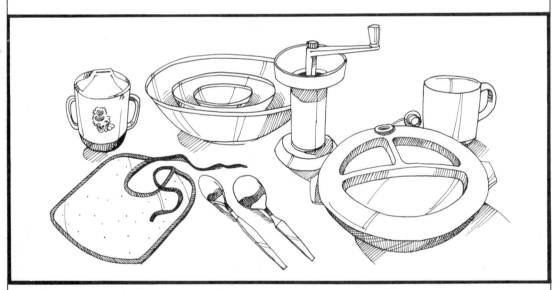

How to introduce solids

• Introduce solid foods while your baby is still getting a substantial amount of her nourishment from breast milk or formula. That way, you can feel comfortable letting her experiment with the new experience of solids. So at first you'll want to offer solids in addition to, not in the place of, breast milk or formula.

• Don't force solid foods on your baby. She'll eat when her body needs them. In fact, the whole goal of introducing solid foods should be to make mealtime an enjoyable, stress-free activity. Leave your baby alone, and she'll eat what she wants to eat.

● Respect your baby as an individual. Even at six months old she'll display preferences and enjoy variety.

● At first, be sure to introduce solid foods one at a time, and then wait a few days after each new food to make sure it doesn't cause an allergic reaction. Avoid stews, soups or multigrain cereals when you're starting out—if your baby has an allergic reaction to one of these, you won't know exactly what food caused it.

Allergic reactions

If your baby begins wheezing or develops rashes, a sore bottom, or diarrhea and you've just introduced a new food in the last day or two, she may be having an allergic reaction. Most food reactions are mild and no cause for alarm. Just make sure you don't give your child that food until she's several months older, and then reintroduce it at first in very small amounts. However, if your child's reaction is severe, or you're in doubt, be sure to contact your physician.

Common sources of food allergies

The most common sources of food allergies in infants are cow's milk and egg whites. In addition, wheat, corn, pork, fish, shellfish, onions, citrus fruits, nuts, and strawberries can also cause allergic reactions in some babies. In general, you may want to delay offering any of these foods to your child until she's at least a year old. And certainly, if you have a family history of allergies to any of these foods, you'll want to consult your physician before you offer it to your child.

Other foods to avoid

For other reasons you should also avoid introducing any of the following foods to an infant:

● **Honey,** which is possibly connected to the occurrence of a disease called infant botulism. Do not offer it during your baby's first year.

● **Nuts and popcorn** or any other food that could cause your infant to choke.

● **Heavily sweetened foods** such as soda pop, lemonade, baby food desserts.

● **Spicy or salty foods.** Your infant probably doesn't have as highly a developed sense of taste as you do, so you don't need to season her food.

Feeding schedules

● Start offering your baby solid foods once a day (midmorning or midafternoon is ideal—you won't be distracted by the rush of family mealtimes).

● After a couple of weeks, increase the frequency to twice a day.

● After about a month of trying solids, start offering your child solid foods *in between* a nursing or bottlefeeding session—she'll have a better appetite for them while still not being ravenously hungry. After she's had enough of the solids, offer her more milk as a "topper."

● At this point, observe your child's appetite and degree of satisfaction with what you're offering her. If you patiently allow her to set the pace and if you make sure what she needs is offered when she seems to want it, she'll gradually wean herself from entirely "milk meals" to regular meals with the family.

How much food?

● Introduce solids to your child in small amounts, like 1 to 2 teaspoons (5 to 10 ml.), until she gets used to the taste and the practice. Make the consistency of the food rather watery by diluting it with breast milk or formula.

• Increase the amount gradually to 4 to 6 tablespoons (60 to 90 ml.) as she becomes more accomplished at eating and as her appetite for solids increases. (A small jar of commercial baby food contains 8 tablespoons—128 ml.—of food.) Here are rough guidelines for the first year of life:

AGE	AMOUNT PER DAY
6 to 7 months	Breast milk or iron-fortified formula Baby rice cereal mixed with breast milk or formula (up to 8 tbsp.) Non-citrus juice (2-4 oz.) Strained fruits and cooked vegetables (up to 8 tbsp.)
8 to 9 months	Breast milk or iron-fortified formula Baby cereal mixed with breast milk or formula (8 tbsp.) Juices, including citrus juices (2-4 oz.) Strained to finely chopped fruits and cooked vegetables; bite-size pieces when ready (6-8 tbsp.) Strained meats and pureed egg yolks (no whites until one year old)
10 months to 1 year	Breast milk or iron-fortified formula Baby cereal mixed with breast milk or formula (6-8 tbsp.) Juice (2-4 oz.) Mashed or bite-size fruits and cooked vegetables (6-8 tbsp.) Ground or chopped meat and meat substitutes, like egg yolks (1-2 oz.) Potato and whole grain or enriched grain products

• Never force your child to eat or try to slip in "one last bite" when it's clear she's had enough.

• You'll be able to tell when your child is finished with her meal by her behavior: she'll turn her head away from the spoon or close her lips tightly and refuse to take anything more into her mouth. Crying, gagging, or spitting the food out may suggest your baby doesn't want more food, but these signs may also indicate that she hasn't quite learned how to eat solids yet, or that your feeding technique could be improved.

How to spoon feed

A breastfed or bottlefed baby knows of feeding entirely in terms of sucking, so give her some time to catch on to how to use a spoon. The best way to introduce it is by putting a small dab of food on the tip of the spoon (be sure to use a small baby spoon or a demitasse spoon), placing it just between the baby's lips, and then letting her suck the food off. She'll soon become experienced enough to receive the food from the spoon directly into her mouth.

A note about messes

Babies are messy eaters. The more you try to fight that, the unhappier mealtimes will become for both you and your child. So be prepared and you'll be freed from much of the dismay. You may want to line the floor around your child's eating area with newspapers. A bib on your baby and an apron on yourself helps. Most important, though, is a relaxed attitude and an eye for making mealtimes enjoyable, whatever the mess.

What kinds of foods

Mashed ripe bananas or a little rice cereal mixed with breast milk or formula are the two most commonly recommended foods to first introduce to a baby. Iron-fortified cereals are recommended to meet your baby's iron needs. (Don't put foods like cereals into her bottle, unless your physician has specifically advised you to do this. This teaches babies to drink solids, which is not a good practice.)

Once your child becomes comfortable eating bananas and rice cereal, you can expand her menu in a number of directions:

- **Various cereals,** such as barley, millet, or oatmeal, moistened with breast milk or formula.
- **Mashed white potatoes,** mixed with breast milk or formula.
- **Sweet potatoes or winter squash,** mashed and moistened with apple juice or water.
- **Other vegetables,** such as cooked carrots, skinned beets, peas, and spinach, mashed or pureed.
- **Fruits,** such as apples, peaches, and pears, that are peeled, then cooked into a sauce or pureed.
- **Pureed, mashed or finely chopped meats,** moistened with a little water or juice from the meat.
- **Egg yolk,** cooked and mashed with a little water, breast milk, or formula. (Be sure to avoid offering egg whites until your baby is at least one year old. Egg whites are one of the most common sources of allergies when introduced too early.)

Once your baby has comfortably gone this far and is happily eating, you can offer her many of the foods that the family is eating. Experiment carefully, however, with gas-producing foods like broccoli, cabbage, and onions.

Vitamin supplements

The best way for your baby to get the vitamins she needs is through a balanced diet of nutritious foods. Once she starts eating a variety of solid foods, you can discontinue any vitamin supplements you're giving her.

Preparing baby foods at home

No one will disagree that home-prepared baby foods are cheaper and fresher than commercially prepared foods. With a baby food grinder or a food processor, you can quickly turn almost any of the foods you eat into something your baby will enjoy. See p. 62 for more on making baby food at home. Vicki Lansky's *Feed Me! I'm Yours* (Meadowbrook, 1974) offers many more suggestions.

Commercial foods

Commercially prepared baby foods are convenient and sterilized, and they frequently contain vitamin and mineral supplements. Although most manufacturers have removed unnecessary additives, you'll still want to check the labels to make sure there's no added salt, sugar, or other preservatives.

It's generally recommended that you use a jar of baby food within one to two days of opening it. Don't feed your baby directly from the jar, since the saliva from your baby's mouth will hasten the growth of bacteria in the food.

Warming baby foods

It's not necessary to heat foods for your baby; in fact, she may prefer them at room temperature. If you do want to warm her baby food, however, you can set a jar of food in a pan of water on the stove or heat the food in a microwave (but be careful not to overheat it). You can also buy a plastic feeding dish that you fill with warm water to heat the food.

Finger foods

Once your baby has a few teeth and has developed the necessary hand coordination, she'll want to try feeding herself. This usually happens at around eight to twelve months, although often she'll be able to handle crackers or hard, dry toast a little earlier. Below is a list of finger foods that are nutritious, easy to handle when offered in small bites, and appropriate for stomachs just getting used to solid foods.

Chopped chicken livers
Chicken shreds
Boned fish
Egg yolks
Peanut butter on whole wheat toast
Hamburger
Diced beef, veal, lamb

Bananas
Cooked pieces of apples, pears and
  peaches
Ripe avocado
Mashed potatoes
Lima beans
Tofu (soybean curd)
Sugarless dried cereal

PREPARING BABY FOODS

WHAT YOU NEED TO KNOW

- For obvious reasons, prepare the foods on a very clean surface (avoid wooden cutting boards that have been used for cutting meat).

- Don't add sugar, salt, or other seasonings to the baby food you make.

- Be sure to freeze foods that will not be used within 24 hours. (Ice cube trays come in handy for freezing individual portions.)

WHAT TO DO

1 First cook the meats, fruits, or vegetables you plan to offer your child. You can use canned fruits and vegetables, but they're not as nutritious as fresh or frozen foods.

2 Puree, grind, mash or finely chop the cooked foods in a blender, food processor, or baby food grinder. Make sure that the texture of the food is right for your beginning eater. If it's too coarse, she might choke. The older your child gets and the more experienced she becomes at eating, the coarser the texture you can offer her.

3 Spoon the pureed food into an ice cube tray and freeze it. When the cubes are frozen, you can store them in plastic bags in the freezer and use them one at a time. (Just reheat them in a pan or in the microwave.)

Chapter 4

YOUR BABY'S SAFETY

Because of improved preventive health care and other advances in medicine, diseases that formerly killed infants have been largely eliminated or controlled. Today, accidents kill more children than the next six causes of death combined, and automobile accidents are by far the leading cause of death and injury to infants.

Your objective should be to provide a safe environment that your child can explore. As a parent, the most important thing you can do is make sure your baby is put into an approved car seat when you travel. It's also important that you anticipate your child's next development, so you can child-proof your house *before* he enters a new stage. On the pages that follow you'll find a complete guide to child-proofing your home, plus information on buying baby equipment.

Newborn babies are totally helpless and need to be protected at all times. As a baby begins to wriggle, roll over, grasp objects, creep, and eventually crawl, accidents tend to happen more often. Children are naturally curious and active, but their balance and sense of danger don't develop until they're older. They need to be able to explore their environment in a safe and carefully supervised way.

Below is a general outline of a baby's typical development during the first year. Details are provided in chapter 5.

Birth through 2 months	Your baby will wriggle and may start to roll over.
3 through 5 months	Your baby will begin to rock and roll over, and he'll start to grasp things and put them into his mouth.
6 through 9 months	Your baby will begin to creep, crawl, pull himself up, and pull everything else down.
10 through 12 months	Your baby will begin to stand, climb, and possibly even walk.

CHILD-PROOFING YOUR HOME

General safety tips

- Cover unused outlets with safety caps. Use safety covers over outlets with electric plugs in them.
- Put bulbs in all empty light sockets.
- Don't let your baby near electrical appliances when they are in use. Always turn off such appliances when they are no longer being used.
- Keep pins, buttons, screws, beads, coins, marbles, and other small or sharp objects out of your baby's reach. It only takes a minute for a crawling or creeping baby to put a button in his mouth and choke. Also, never feed your infant nuts or popcorn.
- Keep scissors, knives, razor blades, tools, and all breakable or broken objects out of your baby's reach.
- Keep all plastic bags and sheets of thin plastic out of your baby's reach. Never cover the crib mattress with thin plastic. Throw out or lock up plastic bags from the dry cleaners.
- Never leave a baby unattended with a balloon. Once a balloon has popped, remove all pieces immediately, so your baby doesn't choke on them.
- Appliance cords, telephone cords, cords from blinds, and other cords or straps can strangle babies. Keep them out of your baby's reach. And watch him carefully when he's playing with a toy that has a cord.
- Never put necklaces, cords attached to pacifiers, or cords of any kind around your baby's neck.
- Make sure there are no used ashtrays, glasses containing wine or other liquor, matches, or cigarette lighters in rooms where your baby is playing.
- Don't smoke while caring for your baby. Cigarettes can burn your child, and the smoke from them can irritate an infant's lungs and make him more susceptible to disease.
- Have smoke detectors in your basement and in the hallways near bedrooms.
- Place guards in front of open fireplaces, heaters, steam radiators, hot air registers, floor furnaces, and riser pumps. Kerosene and space heaters, which can tip over, are very dangerous.
- Keep firearms and ammunition locked up separately at all times.
- Remove sharp-edged furniture from your child's play area. Safety edges made of soft plastic are useful for softening sharp corners on coffee tables or other low furniture. Foam tape can cover the edges of glass tables.

Kitchen or dining room

- Keep hazardous and poisonous substances (see list on p. 67) locked up or out of reach. Use drawer safety latches or cupboard safety latches to prevent your child from opening drawers or cabinets that hold potentially dangerous objects.
- Make sure the garbage pail is inaccessible.
- Be very careful about letting your baby crawl or walk around the kitchen while you're cooking or serving meals. A baby sitting in a baby carrier on a counter may also be spattered by grease or food.
- Turn all pot handles inward so that your child can't pull them off the

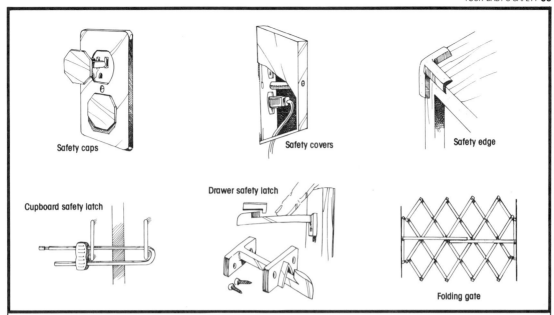

Safety caps

Safety covers

Safety edge

Cupboard safety latch

Drawer safety latch

Folding gate

stove. A good policy while cooking is to simmer foods on the front burners and boil foods on the back burners.

● Never leave the oven door open. And keep your children away from oven doors that are hot to the touch.

● Don't let your child play with knobs on a gas stove. If necessary, remove the knobs.

● Don't drink hot liquids while your baby is in your lap. You might spill them by accident, or the baby's moving arm might tip or knock hot liquid onto himself or you.

● Keep all hot objects and hot liquids out of your baby's reach—and, especially, away from the edges of counters and tables.

● Avoid using tablecloths while your baby is small. Babies love to pull their edges and a child could pull something on top of himself.

Bathroom

● Never leave your baby alone in the bathtub—even for a second.

● Before bathing your baby, always check the bath water to make sure it's not too hot. Turn off the water faucets tightly so that your baby can't open them. Set the hot water heater to 125°F. (51.6°C.) so there's no chance that your baby could be unintentionally scalded.

● Don't let your baby play in the bathroom—there are too many hard objects and slippery surfaces. And a curious child could drown in a toilet bowl. Always keep the bathroom door closed.

● Put medicines and other potentially hazardous materials—e.g., cleansers, cosmetics, and soaps—away immediately after use (see list on p. 67). If the phone rings while you are using such a substance, ignore the call or take the child with you to answer the phone.

● Try to buy medicine in child-proof containers.

● Always check medicine labels for proper dosages before administering them to your child. Never give medicine to a child in a darkened room. Don't give medicine prescribed for one child to another child.

- Don't save "leftover" medications; discard safely any unused part of a prescription.

- Avoid calling the medicine "candy" so that the child doesn't associate the two. A leading cause of poisoning in children are overdoses of good-tasting medicine (e.g., candy-flavored vitamins and aspirin).

Bedroom

- Never leave a baby unattended on a changing table, bed, couch, or other high place from which he might fall. While changing your baby, use a safety strap or keep one hand on the baby at all times. If the phone rings while you're changing the baby, or if you must leave the room, wrap him up and take him with you or lay him down in a crib or playpen.

- Buy only flame-retardant sleepwear for your baby.

- When your baby is able to sit by himself, lower the crib mattress. Set it at its lowest point before the baby can stand.

- Don't leave large toys in a crib or playpen. The baby can use them as steps to climb up and out.

- Place vaporizers and portable heaters beyond your child's reach, and keep them away from your child's bedclothes.

- Put a sticker on your baby's window that would alert a firefighter to the presence of a child in that room.

Stairs

- Keep stairs free of objects that could cause you to fall while carrying your baby. Remove extension cords and scatter rugs. Hold the handrail while going up or down stairs. Don't wax stairs.

- When your baby starts to move around, you should barricade tops and bottoms of staircases with safety gates. Babies learn to go up before they learn to go down.

- Put a railing on open stairs. Make sure that the gaps between the bars of the railing are not wide enough to trap a baby's head.

Outside

- Don't allow your child in the yard when you are using power equipment such as lawn mowers or snow blowers.

- Don't leave a child alone in the yard where he could crawl or walk into the street. Keep an eye on him to make sure he doesn't pick up dangerous objects or put them in his mouth.

- Be very careful of exposing infants and small babies to direct sunlight. Build up your child's exposure—in the beginning, two minutes of sun a day, front and back, should be the maximum exposure. Gradually increase the exposure time until after a month it equals 45 minutes. Try not to expose your baby to midday sun. The safest time for exposure is before 10 a.m. and after 3 p.m.

Poisonous substances

Here are some tips on avoiding or handling an accidental poisoning in your home.

- Make sure the number of the local poison-control center is posted near your telephones.

- Keep syrup of ipecac on hand. It's used to induce vomiting for some types of poisonings; however, always check with your poison-control center before using it. (See p. 121.)

- All poisonous substances should be kept out of your child's reach, preferably in a locked container or cupboard. Use drawer safety latches, cupboard safety latches, or strapping tape to prevent your child from opening drawers or cupboards that hold potentially dangerous substances. And make sure you keep those drawers and cupboards closed, or the safety latches will do no good.

• Keep all hazardous materials and medicines in their original containers, with their original labels.

• When discarding containers that have held hazardous substances, put them in the garbage with a secure lid or remove them from the house altogether. An empty bottle of cleaner thrown into an accessible wastebasket is easy prey for a crawling baby.

• Don't let your baby chew on newspaper, magazine, or book pages. Some newsprint may be toxic.

• Children love to unwrap presents, but don't let them chew on the ribbons. The dye in some ribbons may be toxic.

• Don't let your child chew on window sills, porch steps, bars on iron gates, or any other surfaces that may have been painted with lead paint. When painting indoor surfaces and toys, use unaltered lead-free paint.

Below is a list of household products and other substances that are potentially poisonous. This is only a general list. Many other substances, such as cosmetics, perfumes, and mouthwashes, may be poisonous as well.

Aspirin and other drugs	Insect and rat poisons
Liquid furniture and auto polish	Lye, alkalies for cleaning drains, bowls, ovens
Leaded paint	Plant sprays and weed killers
Oil of wintergreen	Detergents
Cleaning fluids and powders	Washing soda
Ammonia	Wax remover
Bleach	Borax
Metal polish	Lighter fluid
Mothballs	Turpentine
Shoe polish	Paint thinner
Insecticides	Car cleaner
Kerosene, gasoline, benzene, and cleaning fluids	Antifreeze

Poisonous plants   Many household and garden plants are poisonous. Teach your child never to eat or suck on any part of a plant not commonly used as food. Nibbling on leaves, sucking on plant stalks, or drinking water where plants have been may cause poisoning. Below is a list of poisonous plants; some parts or all of the plant may be poisonous.

Dieffenbachia	Oleander
Caladium	Elephant ears
Some philodendrons	Bulbs from hyacinth, narcissus, and daffodils
Poinsettia	Ivy
Holly berries	Hydrangea
Swedish ivy	Laurel
Lily of the valley	Yew
Rhododendron	
Deadly nightshade	

BABY EQUIPMENT

Car seat

As noted earlier, auto collisions are the most common cause of injuries or death in childhood. In the past few years, more and more laws have been passed that require the use of an approved car seat from birth to four years. Not without good reason: safely constructed and properly anchored restraints have been shown to reduce the probability of a fatal injury in auto accidents by well over 95 percent.

When a car hits another object or stops suddenly, all the occupants continue to move forward at the same speed at which the car was traveling—until something stops them. Unrestrained children become flying missiles. Don't imagine that you can protect your baby by holding him snugly in your arms. Even if you are strapped in, tests have shown that your baby would be "torn" from your arms by the force of the impact. And if you strap your infant in with *your* strap, your own weight, increased by the crash forces, can press the belt deeply into the child's body, causing serious or even fatal injuries.

Children need to have crash forces spread evenly over their fragile bodies, which is exactly what car seats are designed to do. So, do your child a favor and use the car seat fom his first ride home from the hospital. If your baby is used to riding in a safety device from infancy, he will continue to accept restraint as a matter of course.

Here's what you need to know about car seats and auto travel with infants.

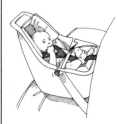

• Child-restraint seats must be installed and used exactly as recommended by the manufacturer. Some seats can be used only for infants or toddlers, while others can be converted for dual use.

• Infants should ride in a semireclined, backward-facing restraint anchored to the seat by a lap belt. In case of an accident, the baby's sturdy back, rather than his delicate chest and abdomen, absorbs the crash forces.

• When your baby is old enough to sit alone and weighs about 20 pounds (9 kg.)—often at nine or ten months of age—he can be moved to a forward-facing position in the car seat.

• The back seat is safer than the front seat, and the center of the vehicle is safer than the sides.

• If child restraint is not available, use a lap belt. Make it as snug as possible; position it across your baby's thighs and hip bones, but don't strap yourself into the same belt.

• Don't carry heavy or loose objects unsecured inside a vehicle, and don't let your children play with pens, pencils, or other sharp or metal objects while the car is moving.

• Never leave a child unattended in a car. The inside of a car can get quite stuffy in hot weather, and when your child is old enough she could unintentionally set the car in motion.

Crib

Since your baby spends so much time in it (much of it unattended), possibly no piece of baby equipment is as important as the crib. New Consumer Product Safety Commission regulations about cribs went into effect in 1974. Make sure any crib you buy, new or used, meets these standards, described on the following page.

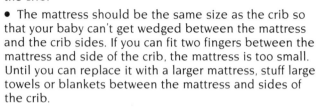

• The space between crib bars must be 2⅜ inches (5.9 cm.) or less (roughly the width of three adult fingers) so that your baby won't get his head caught between them. Be careful of loose bars that could come out, leaving dangerous gaps. Make or buy a crib bumper to tie around the inside perimeter of the crib.

• The mattress should be the same size as the crib so that your baby can't get wedged between the mattress and the crib sides. If you can fit two fingers between the mattress and side of the crib, the mattress is too small. Until you can replace it with a larger mattress, stuff large towels or blankets between the mattress and sides of the crib.

• The minimum height from the top of the railing to a mattress set at the lowest level should be 22 inches (55 cm.).

• When lowered, sides should be 4 inches (10 cm.) above the mattress. Sides should be operated with a locking, hand-operated latch that can't be easily or accidentally released.

• Metal hardware should be smooth—no rough edges or exposed bolts.

• If you paint your crib, use a lead-free, nontoxic paint.

• When the height of the crib side is less than three-quarters of your child's height, it's time to move him to a bed.

Stroller or carriage

• Strollers and baby carriages should have safety belts to prevent a child from standing up and to keep his weight properly centered.

• Look for a wide wheel base and wheels that are large in diameter.

• On a folding stroller, see that there is an adequate lock to prevent accidental collapse. Look for the safety catch.

• Check to be sure that there are no sharp edges or scissor-like mechanisms.

• Make sure there's enough extra headroom when the canopy is down so your baby won't outgrow the stroller too quickly.

Backpack

A backpack is a great way to carry your baby, either outside or in the house. But don't use one before your baby is four to five months old, when his neck will be strong enough to withstand jolts.

• Choose a carrier to match your baby's size. Leg openings should be neither so big that the baby could slip through nor so small that his legs become chafed. There should be enough depth to support the baby's back. Many models have adjustable straps and an inner seat.

• Look for a carrier made of sturdy material, with strong stitching and heavy-duty snaps. Also look for padded covering over the metal frame near the baby's face.

• Make sure there are no joints that may close, pinch, or cut your baby. See that there are no sharp points or edges, and no rough surfaces.

• Always use safety straps.

• When leaning over or stooping, bend from your knees, not from your waist, to prevent the baby from falling out.

Infant seat

- Look for a wide base for stability.
  - Check supporting devices that snap on the back of a baby carrier. Some can pop out, causing the carrier to collapse.
  - Never use a baby carrier as a car seat, and stay within arm's reach of your baby when the carrier is on a table, counter, couch, chair, or other high place. Avoid putting it on slippery surfaces, like glass tabletops.
  - Always use a safety strap while the baby is in a carrier. If the carrier doesn't have one, attach your own.

Front carrier

A soft front carrier is a wonderful way to transport your new baby. Your baby will enjoy the warm containment it provides, and you'll like the freedom it gives you to move about, both indoors and outdoors.

- Make sure the carrier is made of strong fabric and has well-constructed seams, padded leg holes, and padded shoulder straps.
- Be sure there is no way for a baby to slip through the side or leg openings.

High chair

Once your child starts to eat solid foods and can sit up without support (usually between six and eight months), you'll be using a high chair regularly.

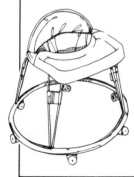

- Buy a chair with an adjustable tray and footrest to adapt to the baby's growth.
- Choose a wide base for stability. Also make sure that the high chair has a safety strap that is not attached to the tray, and always use it.
- Avoid hardware with rough edges or sharp points.
- Check the tray to see that it is properly latched to both sides. The tray should have a strong tray latch.
- Supervise the child closely when he is in the chair. Don't let other children pull on the chair or climb on it when the baby is in it, and don't allow a child to climb in or out of the seat alone.
- Situate the chair in an area free of traffic—i.e., away from doorways, refrigerators, ranges, and other equipment.

Walker

Walkers are a great way for babies to get exercise and protect themselves while they're learning to walk. Be sure, however, to select and use a walker carefully and properly.

- Select a walker on which the wheel base is wider and longer than the frame. Small, flimsy wheels and a narrow base can contribute to tipping. Be sure the seat is made of sturdy material.
- Look for protective covers on coiled springs and hinges. Locking devices and screws should have no sharp edges or points.
- Even walkers that have been redesigned to meet the most current safety and stability criteria will tip over when subjected to enough force. A child in a walker needs constant supervision.

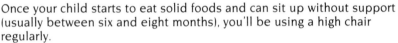

• Walkers can easily roll down stairs, so block off all stairways when the child is in a walker. Also, block off heating vents and radiators during the heating season so your child won't burn himself.

• Walkers can tip over when the child maneuvers over thresholds and rugs, so close doors and remove throw rugs that could get in the way.

Play yard or playpen

A play yard (playpen) can be useful when you want to put your child in a safe place so you can run to answer the door. But don't overuse it, since your baby needs to be able to explore his environment. A play yard shouldn't be a substitute for a properly child-proofed house.

• If the play yard is wooden, make sure the side slats are set close together so that the baby can't get his head caught between them (no more than 2⅜ inches—5.9 cm.—apart).

• If the play yard is mesh, check openings in the netting to see that they aren't wide enough for the baby to poke his arms and legs through and get caught. Play yards that have small-weave netting are preferable.

• See that any metal catches are outside the mesh or railing. Also, any mesh models should have a padded rim.

• Make sure that hinges and latches on folding models lock tightly. There should be no scissoring action when the play yard is in use.

• Check for firm floor support to prevent a play yard with legs from collapsing.

• Keep the play yard away from potentially dangerous objects— lamps, cords, glass, blinds, stoves, and heaters, for example. Don't tie toys to play yard railings — a child could strangle himself on the string.

Jump-up harness and wind-up swing

• Read the instructions for hanging the *jump-up* carefully; if it's not secured properly, it could come loose while the baby is inside.

• The *swing* should be sturdy and have no loose screws or bolts. The seat and cross-bar should be strong and well constructed to prevent the baby from falling forward.

• Check for potentially dangerous springs that might injure your baby's fingers.

• Position the swing or harness away from traffic areas in the home and away from potentially dangerous objects that a baby might reach for, such as electrical appliances, heaters, and glasses.

• Check leg and side openings to make sure that a baby couldn't slip through them.

• A baby in a wind-up swing or harness should be supervised at all times. Babies have been known to tip them over.

BABYSITTERS

You'll no doubt use the services of a babysitter at some time during your child's first year, and you'll probably be nervous the first few times you leave your baby with someone else. To help ease your mind, make sure any babysitter you hire has had experience and feels comfortable with small babies. Observe how your sitter handles the baby, and give your baby time to become comfortable with your sitter.

Here's some other general, commonsense advice about babysitters:

• Always leave the phone number(s) where you can be reached and the time you'll be home. (Pre-printed forms help you organize this information.)* If you can't be reached, check in periodically and leave the phone number of someone the sitter could contact in case of an emergency. Check with that person ahead of time to make sure that he or she will be home.

• Show the sitter where you keep the phone numbers of your doctor, hospital, ambulance, police, and poison-control center.

• Check whether the sitter knows what to do in case of emergencies such as falls, choking, and fire. Have a first-aid chart handy for the sitter to refer to in case of an accident. Show the locations of your fire exits. Review these procedures with the sitter, just to make sure. If the sitter does not know, instruct him or her carefully.

• When using a babysitter for the first time, it's a good idea to have him or her come early (or a day before) so that you can review safety procedures.

• Inform the sitter of any allergies your child may have. If the sitter needs to administer medicine to the child, be sure he or she knows the correct dosage and knows not to give medicine to the child in a darkened room.

• Inform your sitter of any special precautions that should be taken with the baby (e.g., doors that should be kept closed).

*One such product, *Dear Babysitter* by Vicki Lansky (Meadowbrook Press, 1982), combines a refillable pad with a handbook for sitters that includes a first-aid section and spaces for permanent information sitters might need.

Chapter 5

YOUR BABY'S DEVELOPMENT

The first year of life is an exciting time for parents. You watch and help your child as she gradually changes from a helpless newborn—controlled by instincts, reflexes, and basic survival needs—to a toddler with a personality all her own—actively exploring her environment, communicating, solving problems, and already beginning to become independent in many ways. The first year is a time of rapid change for your child and your family, with new experiences taking place and new skills developing nearly every day.

Your child is an individual; no one else is quite the same. Although children develop within the same general sequence, each child's timing is unique. She will spurt ahead in one area of development, while standing still in others; then she'll "catch up" in these areas, while she practices and perfects the earlier skills. The milestones of development presented in the following pages are only meant to suggest what a "typical" pattern of development might be. Do not be alarmed if your infant strays from this pattern during her first year.

All children have a drive to learn, to explore, and to grow. All they need is a safe, loving, interesting environment with as few limitations as possible on their activity. As they mature, their tools for learning will change and their skills will increase in complexity. Formal "teaching" is seldom necessary at this stage. The activities that your child undertakes, the games that you naturally play, and eventually her imitation of the people around her will "teach" her what she needs to know.

Enjoy watching your child. Observe her preferences, cues, responses, and early attempts to initiate interaction. Respond to these and allow her time to respond to you. Try often to see the world from her perspective, and you will be able to take part in her development.

BIRTH THROUGH TWO MONTHS

Your baby's first two months are dominated by her basic physical and emotional needs. At first it seems that all she does is eat and sleep. Awake or asleep, most movements are in relation to the reflexes discussed in the first chapter. During her brief periods of alertness, she'll begin to use her basic senses—one sense at a time—to learn about herself and anything that enters her environment. But her inability to control her movement severely limits her exploration of her surroundings.

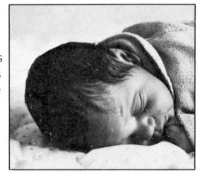

At this age, your baby does not know that there are objects or people separate from herself. Everything is part of her world. After several months of experience with her own body and the world beyond it, however, she'll gradually discover that her toes and fingers feel and taste different from her mother's fingers or a toy, and that her fingers are always with her while other objects come and go.

The basis for your baby's future confidence, relationships, trust in the world, and even independence is now developing. She learns gradually that her needs are met regularly and lovingly, that her world is a safe, secure, fairly predictable place. This sense of security will eventually enable her to explore further, to try something new, to feel comfortable in an unfamiliar place, and to continue to grow and develop in all ways.

FIRST MONTH	
Developmental milestones	**During the first month, your baby may . . .** • make movements that are mostly controlled by reflexes (for instance, grasping or "stepping") • lift her head briefly when she's on her stomach; otherwise, she can't hold it up without support • make eye-to-eye contact at close range, usually between 8 to 12 inches (20 to 30 cm.) • stare at objects (without reaching for them) and prefer looking at faces and patterns; red and yellow seem to be an infant's "favorite" colors • sleep a lot and be alert for only brief spells each day • begin to be comforted by mouthing and sucking her fist and fingers • show enjoyment by quieting down and possibly producing a short-lived smile • distinguish one or two people by their voices

SECOND MONTH	
Developmental milestones	**During the second month, your baby may . . .** • turn from side to side (active movements may roll her off a bed or table)

- lie in the "fencing" position—one arm straight out, head turned to that side, the other arm flexed up

- have better head control—while she's sitting, she may hold it up unsteadily; on her stomach, she may hold it up for a few minutes

- prefer sleeping on or looking to one particular side

- begin to control her grasp and hold an object for a few minutes

- use only one sense at a time—that is, sucking in bursts, looking during pauses

- prefer looking at faces or moving objects or people, but may still focus her eyes on close objects only

- begin to follow some movements with her eyes

- begin to seek and respond to attention by smiling, making sounds, moving her arms and legs actively

- cry at predictable intervals, make cooing sounds, and generally be interested in sounds

- recognize her mother's voice and handling

- associate some positions and people with certain events (for instance, her mother with feeding)

THREE THROUGH FIVE MONTHS

As periods of alertness increase in length and frequency, your baby will become dramatically more active. She gradually becomes able to grasp objects purposefully and bring them up to her face—to look at and to taste. The characteristics of each object are learned through sensory exploration, especially mouthing. Her developing ability to sit when supported frees her hands and increases her field of vision so she can investigate her surroundings more fully.

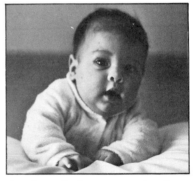

Your baby's social awareness blossoms as she seeks and acknowledges attention by smiling, making noises, and moving her whole body. It is clear that she is becoming more interested in the people and objects around her and that she is enjoying her own activity as well as that of others.

THIRD MONTH

Developmental milestones	**During the third month, your baby may . . .**
	• raise herself up on her forearms (when she's on her stomach) and hold her head up
	• sit supported for a few minutes
	• begin to reach for an object with both hands, bat at things, and kick with force
	• explore a room visually (for light, colors, shapes, patterns) and search for the source of a sound

- smile spontaneously
- look and suck at the same time
- be attentive up to three-quarters of an hour at a time
- begin to show memory of sequences, effects, people (for instance, she may wait for a feeding or bring her body up compactly when lifted)
- use a variety of movements and expressions to indicate her moods and needs
- make sounds in response to talking and singing

FOURTH MONTH

Developmental milestones	During the fourth month, your baby may . . .

During the fourth month, your baby may . . .

- roll from back to side or from stomach to side or back
- sit supported, with her head steady, for ten to fifteen minutes
- push herself straight up from her stomach
- look at and play with her own hands
- reach for (and possibly miss), grasp, hold, and release objects with her hand
- put everything in her mouth
- splash in the bath
- turn her head and eyes to look in all directions, watch moving adults, or locate the source of a sound
- begin babbling and practicing sounds
- laugh
- become attached to one object or toy
- discriminate among faces and know her mother
- be alert for at least one hour at a time and have sustained interest in details
- anticipate a feeding with increased activity and enjoy eating as a social and play time; she may not require a night feeding

FIFTH MONTH

Developmental milestones

During the fifth month, your baby may . . .

- move by rocking, rolling (stomach to back, back to side), twisting, and kicking
- sit propped, with her back firm, for up to half an hour
- be easily pulled to a stand
- reach for and grasp an object smoothly
- wave and raise arms in anticipation of being picked up, and cling when held
- bring her feet to her mouth and suck on her toes
- make sounds to herself, her toys, or her mirror image, and babble to get attention
- show fear, disgust, or anger by making sounds
- awaken at dawn, ready and eager to play
- be alert for one to two hours at a time, resisting interruptions in play

SIX THROUGH NINE MONTHS

Your baby's world is significantly enlarged now that she's beginning to propel herself from place to place by rolling, creeping, and eventually crawling. If she is allowed to move freely in a baby-proofed environment, she will begin to investigate your house or apartment. Few objects will escape her insatiable curiosity. She'll begin to experiment, moving and looking at things in different ways, squeezing, poking, and still tasting everything.

Increasingly, your baby will learn not only by doing, but by watching and imitating others. She has to learn that her parents exist, even when they're out of sight. And she is beginning to perceive and respond to others' mood swings.

As tiny as she seems, in many ways your baby is already starting to become an independent person. She has a distinct personality and distinct likes and dislikes; she is able to move away from the comfort of her caretaker's lap; and she is even beginning to feed herself.

	SIXTH MONTH
Developmental milestones	**During the sixth month, your baby may ...** • roll from back to stomach • sit unsupported for a short time, with her head well balanced and her hands free • love to stand (with lots of support) and bounce • begin to drop things from her high chair, look for them, and cry for others to pick them up • transfer a toy from hand to hand and rotate her wrist to turn and manipulate the toy; want to handle all food and utensils • repeat combinations of sounds ("da-da-da"), watch mouths closely, and try to imitate inflections • show enjoyment of music by humming, swaying, or bouncing • babble, varying pitch, volume, and speed • watch and play with a brother or sister • have memory of her mother, knowing she exists when not seen • show her own individual style in activity level, amount of sleep she requires, and food preferences
	SEVENTH MONTH
Developmental milestones	**During the seventh month, your baby may ...** • creep on her stomach (first backward, then forward) and try to crawl • explore her own body parts

- carry a toy in her hand most of the time
- love noisemaking objects (she may bang blocks on floor or shake things)
- say several syllables (for instance, "ma," "mu," "da," "di," "ba") and use different ones in the same breath
- want to be included socially
- show increasing dependence and fear of separation; fear strangers
- show tension and irritability before a big developmental step (like sitting or crawling)
- dislike having a familiar toy removed and resist pressure to do something she doesn't want to do
- want to help in feeding—exploring foods with her hands, smearing them into her mouth, closing her lips on a spoon to remove food, and holding and playing with a cup and spoon

EIGHTH MONTH

Developmental milestones	During the eighth month, your baby may ...
	<ul><li>crawl</li><li>learn to pull herself to a standing position, discovering which furniture is stable in the process</li><li>get herself into a sitting position, and use her hands to get herself up</li><li>empty cabinets, drawers, bookshelves</li><li>push away unwanted objects</li><li>put an object into a container and shake it</li><li>pick up a small object with her thumb and two forefingers</li><li>hold a bottle to drink</li><li>babble with a variety of sounds, inflections, and two-syllable utterances; she may shout for attention</li><li>listen selectively to familiar words and begin to recognize some</li><li>repeat sounds or movements she has already made</li><li>respond to cues of upcoming events (for instance, she may blink before a cup hits the floor or cry when her mother puts on a coat to leave)</li><li>solve simple problems, like pulling a string to get the toy that's attached</li><li>resist bedtimes and naps</li></ul>

NINTH MONTH

Developmental milestones	During the ninth month, your baby may ...
	<ul><li>stand briefly, when her hand is held</li><li>sit steadily alone and pivot a quarter of the way around</li><li>grasp a small object with her thumb and index finger (in pincer fashion)</li><li>put her fingers into holes</li><li>pass an object from one hand to the other</li><li>be able to finger-feed herself bits of food and drink from a cup with help</li></ul>

- understand and respond to one or two words, besides her name, and be able to carry out simple commands ("no-no," "wave," "clap," "get me the ...")
- look with interest at pictures in a book
- perform for home audience and repeat actions if applauded or laughed at
- prefer watching children to watching adults
- begin to show persistence
- enjoy nursery games, respond to them, and remember a game from the previous day
- fear bathing, heights, separation from her mother in a strange place
- begin to evaluate and respond to others' moods

TEN THROUGH TWELVE MONTHS

These months are a time of transition for your child as she begins to change from an infant to a toddler and from a babbler to a talker. She is starting to learn rules of acceptable and safe behavior and to seek social approval. Gradually, she has refined the use of her hands so that they allow her to use other objects as tools.

The imitation of actions and sounds is developing into the imitation of words, as your baby begins to bring the level of the words she can *say* up to the level of the words she can *understand*. Your baby's self-confidence and assertiveness grow as she acquires more self-help skills. She is on her way to becoming a fully functioning, competent, self-assured person.

TENTH MONTH

Developmental milestones	During the tenth month, your baby may ...
	- stand, for a few moments, with little support - cruise along furniture - climb on chairs - walk with help - lift her leg to help in dressing - carry an object in each hand and dangle an object from a string - hold and bite a cookie, finger-feed herself an entire meal - say "dada" and "mama" (but may not understand them as specific names) - understand and obey some simple commands - imitate nonspeech sounds (cough, tongue click) - imitate actions, remember them, and repeat them later - remember where unseen toys are

- become self-conscious and sensitive to social approval or disapproval
- develop a sense of identity and possession, and show tenderness to stuffed animals and other toys

ELEVENTH MONTH

Developmental milestones

During the eleventh month, your baby may . . .
- walk, holding on to one or two hands
- stand much of the time, without assistance
- climb up stairs (and have trouble coming down)
- use two hands at the same time for different functions (for instance, supporting herself and picking up a toy)
- experiment with dropping and picking up objects
- try the same activity with each hand or with each side of her body
- help more actively in dressing—pulling off a sock, putting her foot in a shoe
- hold a cup with both hands and bring a spoon to her mouth
- explore containers by lifting their lids, putting objects in and taking them out, looking inside
- understand much more than she can say
- mix a word into her babbling or use one word to express a whole thought (for instance, "cookie" might mean "I want a cookie")
- be very dependent on her mother, imitate family members constantly, and play actively with her father
- be shy with strangers and play alongside, but not with, another child
- resist and test limits, seek approval

TWELFTH MONTH

Developmental milestones

During the twelfth month, your baby may . . .
- walk with a wide-legged gait, but may prefer crawling
- get to a standing position from a squat, pivot a quarter of the way around, and lower herself to a sitting position
- use one hand more than the other in reaching, thumbsucking, and finger-feeding; she may use a spoon, spilling often
- hold a crayon to make marks
- push cars and balls, and give a toy to an adult on request
- bang toys or objects together
- stack blocks
- cooperate in getting dressed
- use trial and error to solve problems
- turn into a very picky eater and become more negative (especially at meals and naptime)
- give affection to people and objects
- have renewed fear of strangers and strange situations

TOYS FOR THE FIRST YEAR

To an infant and toddler, everything is a toy. Fingers and toes, crib rungs, buttons and strings on clothing, people and pets, household objects and even pieces of lint are toys. A child's play is her work. Her task is to learn about herself and her world, and her toys are the materials that she learns with.

Since your child will play with anything within reach (and things you thought were out of reach), it is your job to be sure that her reachable world is as safe as possible (see chapter 4 on this subject) and to offer appropriate new challenges. A good and appropriate toy is one that will be interesting at your child's current developmental level — not too difficult or frustrating and not too limited or simple. The charts on the following pages are designed to help you provide toys that fit your child's developmental abilities.

This doesn't mean that you must buy lots of expensive toys. Many parents, in fact, are discouraged to find that their children prefer to play with the boxes that toys came in rather than the toys themselves. You can provide your infant with nearly everything she needs by making toys at home or by simply allowing her to play with common household objects.

- You can suspend some colorful pictures from a clothes hanger to make a mobile.
- When she's starting to play with her own feet, you can sew bells onto her shoes or booties.
- She'll also be fascinated by a set of unbreakable mixing bowls or plastic containers that she can drop things into and dump things out of.
- You can make a simple "clacking" toy by stringing a number of empty wooden thread spools together.

Whether you make or buy toys for your child, here are some considerations you should be aware of:

Safety	Toys and movable parts of toys must be large enough to prevent your child from swallowing them. Pieces must not pull or break off or be able to be chewed off, and toys should not have sharp points or edges. Materials should be labeled nontoxic.
Durability	The toy should not break under the kind of abuse your child can and will give it at this age.
Versatility	A particularly good toy will have many uses at many different ages or developmental levels. There is not just one "right way" to use it. Also, look for toys that stimulate more than one sense. For example, some "clutch" toys now on the market are brightly colored, have faces to look at, are easy to hold, have interesting textures to touch and mouth, and have a bell inside to stimulate hearing (and encourage shaking or turning). Few, if any, toys appeal to all the senses, but many appeal to more than one.

Toy	Age	Developmental activity
Pictures	From birth on	Use pictures to aid the development of your child's visual perception (focus distance, detail, color, image recognition). Attach brightly colored decals, posters or other pictures — especially pictures of faces — to the crib, the wall, or a mobile. At first your baby will focus eight to twelve inches (20 to 30 cm.) away; by four to six months she will be able to focus across the room.
Mobile	Birth to 2 months	A mobile will engage your infant's active interest in her surroundings, especially bright colors and shapes. Look at the mobile from your baby's perspective and place it five to eighteen inches (12 to 45 cm.) from her face. Music or slow movement may also be attractive.
	3 to 6 months	Your child will reach for and grasp her mobile, learning to coordinate hand movements by looking at the target. Move the mobile around so your baby can use her feet as well as her hands to kick, bat, pull, and push it. If the toy makes a noise when your baby moves it or kicks the mattress, she'll be even more interested.
Mirror	2 to 6 months on	A mirror helps your child develop an interest in faces and foster the idea that faces are part of people and that she is a separate person. Hang a small, good-quality, unbreakable mirror on the inner side of the crib, over your baby's head in the crib, or next to the changing table. Your baby will enjoy watching and "talking" to herself, and later she'll enjoy looking at any of the mirrors you have in the house.
Stuffed animals	2 months on	Stuffed animals stimulate lots of activities — an interest in faces (2 months); reaching and grasping (3 to 6 months); and early manipulation of objects and interest in textures (6 to 18 months). A young infant may become attracted to a stuffed animal because of its face. Primarily it's something soft to reach for, grasp, and mouth.
	4 months on	Your child may become attached to a toy, showing affection. A baby will quickly sense what is important to her parents. Since we often hug, talk to, or pay more attention to a stuffed animal than to other toys, your baby may become more attached to this type of toy than to other toys.
Rattle/ squeak toy	2 to 4 months	Rattles, squeak toys, or anything with bells on it give your infant a chance to watch a moving object and look for the source of the sound. Move a brightly colored or shiny rattle or squeak toy slowly past your baby's eyes for her to follow. She will move only her eyes at first, then her head, too. Gently shake the rattle or squeak the toy in front of her, then to each side — your baby will learn to look for the source of the sound.

Toy	Age	Developmental activity
	3 to 7 months	As she gets older, rattles or squeak toys can help your child develop her control of reach, grasp, and release. She'll learn to handle, shake, and bang toys. Hold or suspend the toy where your baby can reach it. Experiment by putting it in front of or to each side of your baby.
Cradle gym or exerciser	3 to 6 months	A cradle gym, which you string over the top of your baby's crib, will provide her with a variety of objects to look at, pull, push, kick at, and grasp.
Ball	3 to 4 months	A brightly colored ball with some kind of noisemaking object inside is best at this age to give your child the chance to watch moving objects and look and reach for the source of a sound. Turn or roll the ball slowly in front of your baby. A soft "clutch" toy designed with places to hold onto is easy to grasp and shake.
	4 months on	When your child has started to roll over, creep, crawl, and finally walk, a ball that's small enough to be held in one hand will be turned, shaken, banged, dropped, rolled, and followed. Again, color and sound add interest.
Stacking rings	3 to 6 months	The removable pieces from a stacking toy are usually brightly colored, easy to grasp, durable, and smooth to mouth. They're perfect objects for the young baby to reach for and handle. They can be strung as a mobile, hung from the side of the crib, or held out for a child to touch.
	9 months on	Later, your child will actually use them as stacking objects, learning to control her hand movements to place the rings precisely in one spot. At first your baby will make a stack of the pieces. When this is no longer a challenge, give your baby the post on which to stack the pieces (with the pieces on), take one off and put it back on. Your baby's curiosity will do the rest.
Board books	6 months on	Your baby may not show much interest in books early on, but they can play a useful role in her language development. Point to pictures, naming and describing things in them, making animal sounds, or telling stories. By nine or ten months, your baby will certainly enjoy a book as an object, turning it over, pulling and moving pages back and forth, mouthing it, and dropping it. Be sure books are sturdy or expendable or both.
Small blocks	5 to 6 months on	This is one of the most versatile, long-lasting toys you will find. Your child will learn to pick up and drop objects, and coordinate hand movements by looking. A

Toy	Age	Developmental activity
		small, brightly colored block is easy to handle and see. Later, she will bang blocks together and on all surfaces. She'll drop small objects into large containers and, eventually, enjoy the challenge of putting a block through a hole in the lid of the container.
	1 to 5 years	Used as stacking objects, blocks will continue to be interesting on and off for years, as your child uses them for building, dramatic play, and learning about size, shape, color, numbers, and so on.
"Nesting" toys	5 to 10 months on	Nesting toys are objects of the same shape but different size (like cups, bowls, cubes, etc.) that can be "nested" (or that fit) inside one another. Using them helps your child develop hand coordination and learn that objects exist when they're not seen. While your baby watches, use a cup to cover up a small toy that she likes, uncover it, and show her where it is. Your baby will soon play the game herself.
Pull toys	8 months to 2½ years	When your baby can crawl, walk along furniture, and finally walk alone, pull toys will give her a sense of power (over objects, specifically) and an extra enjoyment of her new modes of movement. However, most pull toys tip over readily, which frustrates children. Look for sturdy, stable toys, preferably those that are colorful or interesting to look at and make some sound as they move.
Playpen activity box or cube	6 months to 1½ years	An activity box provides objects that can be manipulated, turned, pushed, poked, or hit. This kind of toy has a variety of gadgets, such as doors to open, balls to spin, and telephone dials to turn.

BABY EXERCISES

WHAT TO DO

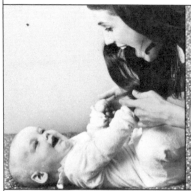 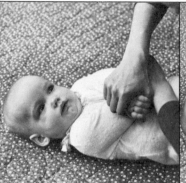 

1 **The Grasp.** (To elicit the grasp reflex.) Put your forefingers in your baby's palms. She will grasp your fingers. Gently pull her hand toward you, and she will pull back on your finger. (Do not attempt to pull her head and shoulders up.) If her hands are closed tighly, pat and bounce her hands to open them.

2 **Arm Cross.** (To relax the chest and upper back muscles.) Place your thumbs in the palms of your baby's hands; she will grasp them. Open her arms wide to the side and then bring them together and cross her arms over her chest. Repeat slowly and gently, using rhythmic movements.

3 **Arm Raising.** (To improve the flexibility of the shoulders.) Grasp your baby's forearms near her elbows. Raise them over her head, then lower them to her sides (as if you're playing "So Big"). Repeat slowly and gently, using rhythmic movements. Then alternate arms, so that one goes up while the other goes down.

  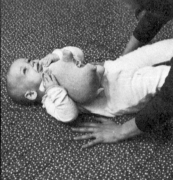

4 **Leg Bending.** (To improve the flexibility of the hips; it may also help your baby pass gas.) With your baby on her back, grasp her lower legs and gently bend her knees up toward her abdomen and chest. Then gently lower her legs until they're straight. You may repeat this several times using both legs, or you may alternate, bending one leg while straightening the other.

5 **Inchworm.** (To bring about the extension of the legs.) With your baby on her tummy, bend her knees under her and tuck her feet close to her body. Hold her feet with your thumbs against her soles. Press and wait. This pressure on her soles will cause her to straighten her legs and move forward like an inchworm.

6 **Baby Bounce.** (For relaxing your baby's whole body.) Place your baby on her back or tummy on a very large, slightly deflated beach ball, a foam rubber pad, the bed, or any soft, bouncy surface. Slowly and gently press on the bouncy area around the baby so that she rocks up and down. Use a rhythmic pattern; as she feels the rhythmic up and down motion, she will relax. Also try patting your baby rhythmically on her stomach, chest, back, arms, and legs.

Chapter 6

MEDICAL CARE FOR YOUR BABY

Making sure your infant is well cared for, both on a day-to-day basis and in the long run, will give him the best chance of continuing a happy, carefree existence throughout his infancy and childhood. Good health now will be a sound foundation for many years to come.

Taking your child in for a series of "well-child" checkups is one of the most important things you can do for him during his first year of life. Regular visits—when your infant is healthy—will help diminish the number of "irregular" visits he'll need because he's sick. And a doctor who sees your infant on a regular basis stands a better chance of being able to pick up on any unusual patterns of growth, development, or behavior, and thus catch problems early.

Being a parent of an infant is not always an easy job, especially if it's your first child, and it's certainly not a natural skill. Regular well-child visits give you the opportunity to share some of what you've experienced and what you've learned with a professional, who can help you in a number of ways— often just by reassuring you that what you're experiencing with your child is quite normal.

On the pages that follow, you'll find out more about the well-child checkups and immunizations recommended for the first year. There's also a section on the development of your child's teeth, a general discussion of how to handle common medical problems, and information on how to treat fever. Finally, this chapter concludes with step-by-step treatments for the illnesses and emergencies that your child *may* face during his first year.

RECOMMENDED CHECKUP SCHEDULE

The American Academy of Pediatrics recommends the following schedule of well-child checkups during the first year. Naturally, if your baby develops health problems that require further attention, you will see health care professionals more frequently.

	By 1 mo.	2 mos.	4 mos.	6 mos.	9 mos.	12 mos.
PHYSICAL EXAMINATION	●	●	●	●	●	●
MEDICAL HISTORY (Health profile)	●	●	●	●	●	●
MEASUREMENTS Height/Weight	●	●	●	●	●	●
Head circumference	●	●	●	●	●	●
TESTS/ SCREENINGS. Vision	●	●	●	●	●	●
Hearing	●	●	●	●	●	●
Blood tests					●	
Urinalysis				●		
Hereditary/ Metabolic	●					
DEVELOPMENT/ BEHAVIOR ASSESSMENT	●	●	●	●	●	●
GENERAL CONSULTATION (As needed)	●	●	●	●	●	●

IMMUNIZATIONS

If you take your child in for the recommended "well-child" checkups, you'll also be making sure he gets the recommended immunizations. During his first year, your child will be immunized against diptheria, pertussis (whooping cough), and tetanus with a series of three shots (called the DPT series). He'll also receive an oral polio vaccine and, most likely, a tuberculosis test. Both the DPT series and the polio vaccine are followed up with boosters in later childhood. (See the recommended schedule below.)

RECOMMENDED IMMUNIZATION SCHEDULE

	2 mos.	4 mos.	6 mos.	12 mos.
DPT (Diphtheria, Pertussis, Tetanus)	●	●	●	
Polio	●	●		
Tuberculosis test				●

An immunization is a preparation of dead or weakened, living organisms. When it's introduced into your child's system, it produces "immunity" to a specific disease by causing his body to build up antibodies or resistance to the organism. These antibodies provide protection, should your child be exposed to the disease in the future.

For a variety of reasons, some infants will have reactions to certain vaccines. The most common and generally quite harmless reactions to the DPT vaccine are general fussiness, a slight fever, and a sore leg at the site of the injection. These usually occur 12 to 24 hours after the injection. You can treat the fever with medication (see pp. 91-93). If your child's leg becomes sore and swollen, you'll want to take extra care when you move it, and you might even want to apply warm washcloths to the swollen area.

More seriously, and *very rarely*, the pertussis component of the DPT vaccine can cause a reaction involving the brain. The consensus of the American Academy of Pediatrics is that the benefits far outweigh the risks. That is, the danger from getting a disease like whooping cough is far more serious than the risks associated with the vaccine.

DENTAL CARE

Your child's first tooth could appear when he's anywhere from three to twelve months old, although around six months is the average. The tooth may simply pop through with no forewarning, or it may give you *plenty* of warning if your child is showing some of the typical symptoms of teething—he drools, fusses, chews on nearly everything in sight, wakes frequently at night, and generally seems bothered by sore, throbbing gums. Some babies even refuse to nurse or take a bottle if their teething is especially troublesome. Each child responds differently. (See p. 124 for more on teething.)

A few more teeth are also likely to erupt during the first year, and a full set of baby teeth will probably be in place by the time your child is three. Here are the average times each baby (or primary) tooth erupts into the mouth, but don't worry if your child's teeth come in earlier or later.

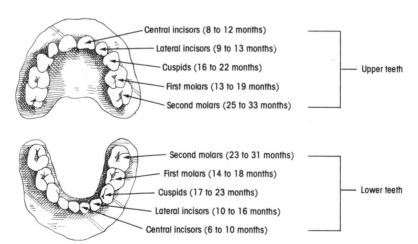

Because healthy baby teeth are essential to the development of your baby's jaw and his later permanent teeth, you'll want to start caring properly for those first teeth even before they start coming in.

• Make sure your child is getting a nutritious diet, including vitamins A, C, and D. Take your child out in the sunshine whenever it is practical. The sun is a natural source of vitamin D.

• Make sure your child is getting fluoride either in the water he drinks (most communities add it directly to the general water supply) or through a mineral supplement. The American Dental Association (ADA) considers fluoride to be the single most important factor in the development of healthy teeth. Because fluoride is most effective when used while teeth are forming, don't wait for the baby teeth to start erupting before adding fluoride to your child's diet. Be sure to administer fluoride dosages correctly, as too much fluoride can cause damage to teeth.

• Once your child is weaned from the breast or bottle, offer him plenty of foods rich in calcium (e.g., milk, cheeses, yogurt)—the primary mineral component of teeth.

• Try to avoid letting your child use the bottle as a pacifier (and don't put him to bed with it.) Oftentimes, an older baby with this habit will demand several refills of milk or juice in a row, especially at night. This habit constantly bathes his teeth in sugary liquids and encourages decay, since milk contains a form of sugar called lactose. The ADA recommends that you start cleaning your child's teeth as soon as they appear. To do this, lay your child on his back so that you have a full view of his mouth. Use a sterile gauze pad or a clean washcloth to wipe his teeth gently, cleaning away any harmful plaque that may have built up during the day.

HANDLING COMMON MEDICAL PROBLEMS

When your infant is sick or hurt, you want to know *quickly* what's best to do. The step-by-step treatments on pp. 95-127 will guide you as you care for your child and will indicate when professional help is necessary. These treatments cover the injuries, illnesses, and emergencies that your child *may* face at one time or another during his first year. You won't find a discussion of diseases that are rare during this period, such as chicken pox or Reye's syndrome.

The treatments in this section are medically sound, but they are not intended to replace professional medical care. Your own doctor may recommend other treatments for any number of reasons. Also, many illnesses vary in their symptoms and effects on different children. Not all issues are black and white, and not all illnesses can be diagnosed with accuracy at one visit. Children often need re-evaluation during the course of an illness to determine its severity. If you have any questions about your child's health or the best way to handle an illness or injury, please call your doctor's office for help or advice. The following symptoms are *always* worth at least a call to your doctor's office:

1. Any clearly life-threatening injury or accident
2. Fever (see pp. 91-93 for guidelines)
3. Serious diarrhea
4. Blood in the urine or stools
5. Sudden loss of appetite that lasts four days or longer
6. Unusual crying, or difficulty in breathing
7. Unusual vomiting
8. Off-color appearance, listlessness, behavior change
9. Convulsions or fits (seizures)

10. Eye or ear injuries or infections

11. Blows to the head that cause unconsciousness (even if brief) or have effects that last longer than 15 minutes

12. Burns with blisters, unusual rashes

13. Indications of pain (favoring a leg, wincing if a spot is touched)

14. Suspected poisoning

15. Swallowing a foreign body

BASIC SUPPLIES

Here's a list of the supplies you should keep on hand—safely, out of reach of your children—for first aid and routine home health care.

Acetaminophen	Nasal aspirator (syringe bulb)
Adhesive tape ½-1 inch wide	Rubbing alcohol
Bandages (adhesive): assorted sizes	Syrup of ipecac
Cotton balls	Thermometer (rectal)
Cotton swabs	Tweezers
Heating pad	Vaporizer
Hot water bottle	Zinc oxide ointment (for diaper rash)

FEVER GUIDE

Parents commonly think of fever as their number-one enemy when their children get sick. This leads them to battle fever aggressively with all the medication and sponge baths they can give, from a mistaken notion that the fever itself is a disease and can easily harm a child.

However, fever is not a disease, but rather is a symptom that shows that a fight against a disease or infection is going on inside the body. In that fight, excess heat is generated in the core of the body and is dissipated to the head and limbs, where it radiates off the skin. In general, pediatricians recommend *not* trying to lower fevers under 102°F. (39.9°C.), and they certainly don't want parents to consider fevers in and of themselves as threats to their child's well-being. Here are some facts that you should know about fever:

Fever levels
- A fever is a temperature of 100°F. (37.7°C.) orally or 101°F. (38.3°C.) rectally.
- The height of a fever does not correlate with the dangerousness of the the disease.
- A high fever is 105°F. (40.5°C.) and above. Harmful effects of fever itself (not just discomfort) do not occur until the temperature reaches 106 to 107°F. (41.1 to 41.6°C.), and they only occur rarely. This is the highest a fever will go in people, since an automatic mechanism limits it at that point.

Fever treatment
- The main reason to treat a fever is to reduce your infant's discomfort and the risk of dehydration. When fever is present, the body loses more fluid than it does under normal conditions.
- You don't need to treat a fever with medication until your baby's temperature goes over 102°F. (38.9°C.), and preferably only then if your child seems uncomfortable. Light clothing, extra fluids, and a pleasantly cool room are better "treatments" unless the fever is higher.

• During your child's first year, you should not give him any medication until you've called your doctor. Don't give baby aspirin to babies under one year of age. Aspirin doesn't come in liquid form, so it's hard to measure accurately. Use acetaminophen drops or syrup (elixir) instead, to ensure more accurate doses. Acetaminophen also comes in a rectal suppository form for use when vomiting makes it difficult for your child to keep the medication down. General guidelines on acetaminophen doses are given below.

RECOMMENDED ACETAMINOPHEN DOSES

The table below shows how many milligrams (mg.) of acetaminophen are recommended for children under one year. It's always best, however, to consult with your physician before administering a dose. Acetaminophen comes in a variety of forms and concentrations, so a dropper-full of liquid made by one manufacturer may not have the same amount of medication as another manufacturer's product. Also, some physicians use your child's weight more than his age in determining how much acetaminophen to recommend.

Age	Amount of medication
Birth to 6 months	40 mg., but call the doctor before giving medication
6 months to 1 year	80 mg., but call the doctor before giving medication

• Carefully measure *and* time the doses of acetaminophen you give your child so you don't overdose him. With acetaminophen, overdosing shows up as nausea, vomiting, and excessive sweating. An overdose of acetaminophen can be fatal. If you suspect that your child has been overdosed, call your doctor or poison-control center immediately.

• Never give more than one dose of acetaminophen in any four-hour period. The medication takes effect in about 30 minutes and lasts for about four hours.

• Begin sponging your infant with room-temperature water (never alcohol) to lower his temperature *only* if his temperature is over 104°F. (40°C.), the fever medications you gave him an hour before have still not lowered his fever, and he seems uncomfortable. If you don't wait an hour after giving medication a chance to work, your child may actually feel chilled from sponging and the fever may rebound when you stop.

• Take your child's temperature before giving another dose of fever medication if he is extremely hot or you are not sure he still has a fever and he's not feeling much discomfort. This way, you can track a rising fever or avoid giving medication your child doesn't need.

• Don't awaken your child for medication or temperature-taking. Sleep is more important than either.

When to contact the doctor's office

• If your infant is less than six months old and has even a low fever, since he may have a serious infection without other clear-cut symptoms.

• If your infant is less than one year old and you think he needs fever treatment, since you shouldn't give fever medications to children under one year of age without first calling the doctor's office.

• If a fever without other symptoms goes over 104°F. (40°C.).

• If a lower fever without other symptoms lasts over 24 hours.

• If your child has a serious underlying disease and has any degree of fever.

Note: If your child has experienced a seizure while he had a fever, your doctor may prescribe a slightly different form of treatment when subsequent fevers occur. It's important to remember, however, that such seizures are rare, and they almost always stop occurring by age six.

HOW TO TAKE TEMPERATURES

It's preferable that infants and toddlers have their temperatures taken rectally. Note that temperatures from rectal readings will be one degree higher than others. Don't leave your child unattended while taking his temperature.

1. Shake mercury level down to below 98.6°F. (37°C.).

2. Lubricate bulb with petroleum jelly.

3. Lay your child across your lap, stomach down. Gently insert the bulb and no more than 1½ inches of the stem into his rectum. Keep your hand against his bottom, to prevent injury in case he wiggles.

4. Take the thermometer out after the mercury has stopped rising for 30 seconds to a minute—this usually takes about three minutes.

5. Wipe off thermometer and read highest level of mercury; record reading.

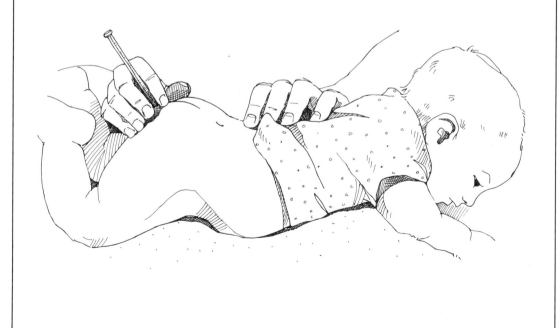

SYMPTOMS INDEX

If you are perplexed about what illness your child may have, try looking up the symptoms you've noticed in the symptoms index. In reading them, see what other accompanying symptoms match (or don't match) your child's. Then make an educated guess about what illness your child has. Again, please don't use the guide to "play doctor," and don't assume that every child with bronchiolitis will have every single symptom listed in that entry. Work closely with your doctor if you have any doubts at all.

ACNE (NEWBORN)

Description: a common condition in newborns that causes the skin to break out in pimples.

What you need to know:

• Newborn acne is common and cures itself. It often appears at three to six weeks of age and disappears or improves significantly within a few days.

Supplies: washcloth, soap, and water

Get professional help if:

• Your infant's acne doesn't clear up in three days with home treatment.

Symptoms:

• blackheads (pimples with dark centers)

• whiteheads (pimples with light centers)

• most often found in oily areas of the skin: around the nose, on the back, near the scalp

What to check:

• Does your infant's acne seem to be spreading rapidly and causing discomfort?

Treatment:

• Wash your newborn's acne gently with a wet washcloth, then dry the area. The clogged pores should open and heal by themselves without further treatment.

BREATHING EMERGENCY

Description: a life-threatening situation resulting from a blocked airway, electric shock, or other condition.

What you need to know:

- Time is critical. Act quickly while someone calls for emergency help.

- If *choking* is the cause, follow the procedures on p. 99 to dislodge the object. Then begin emergency breathing if needed.

- If *electric shock* is the cause, do not touch the child directly if she is still touching the source of the electricity. Turn off the electric current, remove the fuse (or trip the circuit breaker), or stand on a non-conducting mat and push the child away from the source of the current with a non-conducting object like a dry board or rope. *Never* use a wet or metal object.

- Don't tilt the child's head if you suspect a back or neck injury.

- A CPR course prepares you for this emergency.

Supplies: none.

Get professional help if:

- A child's breathing stops. Follow the procedures below until emergency help arrives.

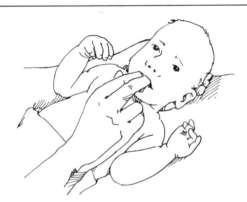

1. Begin while help is coming. Clear the airway. Place child on back, tilt head to point chin up. Listen for breathing. Clear mouth gently with fingers.

2. Cover the mouth and nostrils with your mouth and give four quick puffs. If he still is not breathing, give one breath every four seconds.

3. Continue to breathe for the child. If these procedures do not seem to restore breathing, readjust head tilt to open airway and continue to breathe until help arrives.

BRONCHIOLITIS

Description: inflammation and constriction of the smallest air passages (bronchioles) due to viral infection.

What you need to know:

- Bronchiolitis occurs mostly in infants. Bronchitis is rare.
- It has many of the same symptoms as pneumonia.
- It usually lasts several days, but will resolve by itself.

Get professional help if:

- Symptoms are present, if only to be sure it is bronchiolitis.
- Your baby's lips or skin appear blue, or he seems to be tiring from the increased effort to breathe.
- Your infant refuses fluids for a day or vomits what he drinks.

Supplies: thermometer, prescribed medication, clear liquids, cool mist vaporizer.

Symptoms:

- rapid, shallow breathing
- labored breathing
- wheezing
- fever*
- cough
- loss of appetite

What to check:

- Note temperature three times daily.

Treatment:

- Follow treatment recommended by your doctor. It may include these:
— prescribed medication
— frequent clear liquids
— humidifying the air

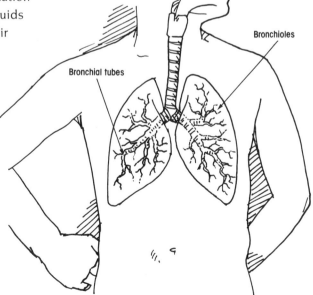

Bronchial tubes

Bronchioles

*See Fever Guide, pp. 91 to 93

CARDIAC ARREST

Description: a life-threatening condition when the heart stops due to breathing emergency or other situation.

What you need to know:	**Get professional help if:**
• Know the A-B-C of cardiopulmonary resuscitation (CPR): Airway, Breathing, Circulation. Get CPR training *before* you need to use it.	• An infant's heartbeat or breathing stops. Follow the steps below while waiting for emergency help.
• If *choking* is the cause, follow procedure on p. 99.	

Supplies: none.

AIRWAY:

1. Determine if infant is conscious by shaking her and trying to wake her up.

2. If you see no response, open airway by gently tilting head back, pointing chin up.

3. Look for chest or stomach movement, feel and listen for breath. If none, begin rescue breathing.

BREATHING:

1. Cover infant's mouth and nose with your mouth to administer breathing.

2. Give four quick puffs, and then one puff every four seconds.

CIRCULATION:

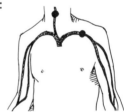

1. Check pulse: an infant's carotid artery is on a line above the left nipple.

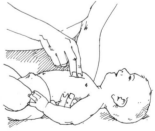

2. For infants, use only the tips of the index and middle fingers to compress the sternum ½ to ¾ inches 80 to 100 times per minute.

CHOKING

Description: a life-threatening obstruction of the airway by an object, food, or croup.

What you need to know:

• The signals of choking: bluish lips, nails, and skin; inability to vocalize, breathe, or cry; high-pitched noises; ineffective coughs.

• Do *not* interfere with your infant *or* call for help if he can still vocalize, cough, or breathe.

• If breathing has stopped, *don't* begin emergency breathing until the airway has been cleared.

Get professional help if:

• Choking lasts more than a minute. Have someone call the rescue squad while you begin emergency procedures.

Supplies: none.

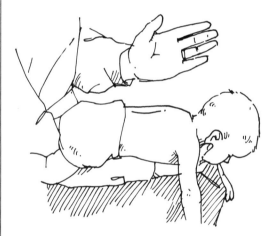

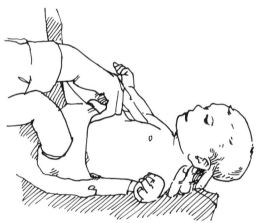

1. Straddle the infant over your arm, face down with his upper chest and jaw in your hand. Give four quick blows between his shoulder blades with the heel of your hand.

2. Quickly turn him up on your other arm, resting it on your leg. With his head lower than the rest of his body, give four quick chest thrusts with two or three fingers. Repeat steps 1 and 2 until the object is dislodged.

3. Once the object has been dislodged, if your baby has stopped breathing or is unconscious, attempt to restore breathing (see p. 96 for details). Call for emergency help.

COLD

Description: a highly contagious viral infection of the nasal and throat membranes; frequently involves ears and chest.

What you need to know:

- Newborns and young infants will often sneeze and bring up mucous that is residual from birth. These are *not* the signs of a cold.
- Colds are most contagious in the first three to four days; symptoms usually subside after the third day.
- Antibiotics don't cure colds and may worsen them or upset an infant's stomach.
- Ear infections are the most common complication.

Get professional help if:

- Your child coughs up green or grey sputum.
- Cold symptoms and fever over 101°F. (38.3°C.) don't improve in four days.

Supplies: thermometer, liquids, nasal aspirator, acetaminophen.

Symptoms:

- congested, runny nose
- red, watery eyes
- sneezing
- dry cough/hoarseness
- breathing difficulty
- listlessness/loss of appetite
- fever*

What to check:

- Check temperature three times a day if the child seems warm or sick.

Treatment:

- Offer water or juice every hour. With infants, draw mucous from nose with a nasal aspirator before feedings and naps.
- Place infant on her side for sleeping.
- Elevate the head of the bed by putting books under the mattress. This helps the mucous drain better.
- Give acetaminophen for fever, after consulting with your physician.

*See Fever Guide, pp. 91 to 93

COLIC

Description: prolonged periods of intense crying in infants, occurring repeatedly over several days, with no apparent cause.

What you need to know:

- It is very common in babies between ages two to four weeks and three months.
- It can be very frustrating to parents because there seems to be no reason for the crying, yet it may continue for hours.
- There's some evidence that colic may be related to a nursing mother's intake of cow's milk.
- Get help early in the course of the problem.

Get professional help if:

- Your baby cries for more than four hours.
- There is fever,* runny nose, cough, vomiting, or other signs of illness.
- Colic is not subsiding by age four months.

Supplies: thermometer, pacifier, hot water bottle or heating pad.

Symptoms:

- spells usually occur in late afternoon, evening, or in the night, often after feeding
- baby may act hungry, but begin crying part-way through feeding
- legs may be drawn up to body and fists clenched

What to check:

- Possible causes of discomfort, such as illness, diaper pin, diaper rash, or hard, pellet-like stools.
- If bottlefeeding, was formula prepared and administered properly, and does the formula flow from the upended bottle at one drop per second?

Treatment:

- It may be necessary to try a variety of methods to soothe your baby; there is no sure-fire treatment and it is possible no method will have results. Be patient and wait it out. Try:

— cuddling, swaddling, soothing talk or music, rocking, walking, backrub, a pacifier, a car ride, "white noise" (like a vacuum cleaner, hair dryer, or washing machine)

— placing your baby on her stomach

— burping your baby

— applying heat to the baby's abdomen.

- Don't overstimulate your baby by too much jiggling or movement.
- If the mother is nursing her child, she should eliminate cow's milk from her diet for two weeks to see if it has an effect.

- Remember that colic is temporary and will disappear with time.
- Get some rest from caring for the infant, even if only for a few hours.
- Discuss your frustration with others.

*See Fever Guide, pp. 91 to 93

CONCUSSION

Description: a blow to the head that can cause minor swelling, unconsciousness and/or amnesia.

What you need to know:

- Head blows are common and are rarely a cause for concern.
- Serious injuries may cause internal bleeding that puts pressure on the brain.
- A good rule: the infant is well if he acts well.

Supplies: ice.

Get professional help if:

- Baby loses consciousness.
- Infant vomits more than twice.
- One pupil becomes larger than the other.
- Baby behaves abnormally: loss of coordination, any seizure activity.

Symptoms:

- symptoms vary according to severity and location of the injury
- minor scalp bleeding and a "goose egg" are common after a bump
- odd behavior or loss of alertness indicate a more serious injury

What to check:

- How does the infant act? If the injury is serious it will produce a symptom.
- Watch baby closely for at least six hours after the injury, even if that requires waking a sleeping infant every two hours.

Treatment:

- Watch infant for signs of serious injury.
- Apply ice to injured area to relieve pain and reduce swelling.
- Treat blows that cause bleeding with ice and pressure. Head cuts bleed easily.

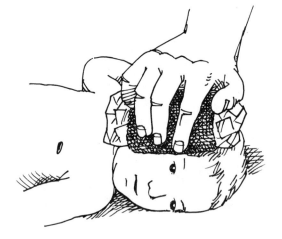

CONSTIPATION

Description: hard bowel movements.

What you need to know:

- Constipation is often overdiagnosed. It may be related to diet or illness, more rarely to a congenital defect of the large intestine.
- Infants differ greatly in their bowel habits; constipation refers to stool *consistency* only, not *frequency*. After one to two months, breastfed babies may have very infrequent bowel movements.

Supplies: Karo syrup, fruit juice, Maltsupex.

Get professional help if:

- Movements seem painful.
- Stools are bloody.
- Infant passes infrequent, but very large stools.
- Constipation recurs frequently.
- The condition does not improve with home treatment.

Symptoms:

- hard stools
- painful bowel movements

What to check:

- Is your child drinking less juice than he normally does? This might lead to constipation.

Treatment:

- Add I teaspoon of Karo syrup or Maltsupex to a bottle twice a day. Or try small amounts of diluted prune juice.
- Consult your physician by phone before giving such home remedies as laxatives, enemas, suppositories, or mineral oil. Do not attempt to stimulate a bowel movement with a rectal thermometer.

CONVULSION (FIT, SEIZURE)

Description: a series of involuntary muscle spasms sometimes associated with periods of temporary unconsciousness, or confusion. In infants, seizures may manifest themselves in more subtle ways.

What you need to know:

• A seizure is not life-threatening. Most seizures result from fever (especially to age three, rarely after age six). Fever-related seizures usually end within five minutes and have no lasting effects.

• Other less common causes include poisoning, severe infection, and epilepsy.

Get professional help if:

• It is your infant's first seizure.

• A seizure lasts more than ten minutes.

Supplies: thermometer, cool water and washcloth, acetaminophen suppository.

Symptoms:

• blue face and lips

• uncontrolled, jerking body movements/rigidity

• vomiting/drooling

• heart palpitations

• headache/stiff neck

• unconsciousness

What to check:

• How does your infant act before and after convulsions?

• How long did the seizure last?

• Did it affect one or both sides of her body?

• Is there fever,* or are symptoms of infection or poisoning present?

Treatment:

• Remove surrounding objects the infant may injure herself on; gently restrain her.

• Make sure her airway is open; give artificial respiration if breathing stops.

• Turn infant on side to prevent choking on vomit or saliva.

• Loosen tight clothing.

• Don't place anything in her mouth (tongue depressors, fingers, liquids, medication) while the seizure is in progress.

• Don't place her in the bathtub; instead, wipe her body with a cool washcloth.

• Once the seizure is over, treat the fever as you normally would, or give acetaminophen suppository.

• Get medical assistance.

*See Fever Guide, pp. 91 to 93

COUGH

Description: a reflexive spasm in response to an irritation of the respiratory system.

What you need to know:
- It can be caused by a variety of conditions, including virus, bacterial infection, asthma, allergy.
- Coughing helps clear the respiratory system of irritants.

Get professional help if:
- Your child is less than three months old and has a persistent cough.
- Breathing is rapid, difficult, or wheezy.
- Fever* is persistent.
- A cough lasts more than ten days.
- A foreign object has been swallowed.

Supplies: thermometer; liquids, such as water and fruit juices; cool mist vaporizer (optional); OTC cough medicine (optional).

Symptoms:
- Coughing itself is a symptom of some other condition.

What to check:
- Try to identify the cause of the cough to decide what treatment to use.
- Check your infant's temperature every four to six hours if he seems warm.

Treatment:
- Treatment will depend on the type of cough.
- Give plenty of liquids to soothe the throat and loosen mucous.
- Vaporizers may soothe irritation with croup and bronchitis.
- In general, use medicine only if coughing is interfering with sleep or making your baby tired. (Consult your physician about what medication you should give.)

*See Fever Guide, pp. 91 to 93

CRADLE CAP (SEBORRHEA)

Description: a harmless skin condition characterized by oily, yellowish scales or crusted patches.

What you need to know:

- It is most common in infants, but occurs to age six.
- Usually it is on the scalp, but may be on the forehead, eyebrows, behind ears, or in the groin area.
- It is often a recurring condition.

Get professional help if:

- The condition persists after several weeks of home treatment.

Supplies: washcloth, soap and water, fine-tooth comb, baby oil, towel.

Symptoms:

- yellowish scales
- crusting patches of skin with slight redness in surrounding areas

What to check:

- Watch for signs of skin infection—children with cradle cap are susceptible.

Treatment:

- Wash the affected area daily with soap and water, using a washcloth.
- Remove scales with a fine-tooth comb.
- For severe cases, rub baby oil into the affected area and cover with a warm towel for 15 minutes. Then work scales loose with a comb and wash away.

CROSSED EYES

Description: inward or outward turning of one or both eyes rather than parallel eye motion.

What you need to know:

• Periodic crossing of the eyes is normal in young infants and should be markedly improved by two to three months.

• Crossing may result from an imbalance in eye muscles or a visual defect such as near- or far-sightedness.

Supplies: none.

Get professional help if:

• Symptoms are present. If there is doubt, see an ophthalmologist. If present, the condition must be treated to prevent permanent damage.

Symptoms:

• one or both eyes appear to be crossed most or all of the time beyond age two to three months (eyes don't "track")

What to check:

• Don't be fooled: the small amount of white in a baby's eyes may create the illusion that they are crossed, especially when he is looking to one side.

Treatment:

• There are no home remedies. If you suspect crossed eyes, have your child examined by an ophthalmologist (even before age six months).

• Doctor's treatment may involve wearing a patch over the "lazy" eye, glasses, or surgery.

CROUP

Description: a barking cough or labored breathing caused by inflammation and constriction of airways.

What you need to know:

- An attack often comes on suddenly (usually at night), for no apparent reason. It requires immediate home treatment.
- Children under age three are most susceptible because their air passages are small.
- If it's severe, an attack requires immediate treatment.
- It is almost always caused by a virus.

Get professional help if:

- Symptoms worsen rapidly and home treatment doesn't ease the condition in 30 to 40 minutes.
- Fever is above 103°F. (39.4°C.).
- Infant turns blue or drools.

Supplies: thermometer, vaporizer, acetaminophen, liquids.

Symptoms:

- a hacking cough that sounds like the bark of a seal or dog
- difficulty breathing air *into* the lungs
- fever*

What to check:

- Don't leave your infant unattended during an attack. Since an attack may occur several nights in a row, watch her closely for three nights; you may want to sleep in the same room if it is convenient.

Treatment:

- While most cases can be treated at home, contact your doctor at the onset of an attack.
- Take your child into the bathroom, close the door, and run hot water to generate steam.
- If condition doesn't improve in 20 minutes, take her into the cool, outside air for 20 minutes. If there is still no improvement, seek help immediately.
- If the doctor determines home treatment is sufficient, put a vaporizer in the room, give acetaminophen and liquids.
- Don't give cough syrup.

*See Fever Guide, pp. 91 to 93

DEHYDRATION

Description: a condition in which there is an insufficient amount of fluid in the body.

What you need to know:
- The most common causes are diarrhea and vomiting.
- Other causes are excessive sweating and urination.
- Body fluids contain important salts and minerals that must be replaced when the child is dehydrated.

Get professional help if:
- Symptoms are severe.
- Your infant is not able to keep down liquids due to vomiting or diarrhea.
- Home remedies don't improve the condition.
- Your child has diabetes and shows signs of dehydration.

Supplies: thermometer; liquids, including flattened carbonated drinks, commercial electrolyte mixes (such as Lytren, Pedialyte), fruit juice.

Symptoms:
- dry mouth
- sunken eyes and fontanel
- drowsiness
- lack of energy
- either dry or doughy-textured skin
- decreased urine output
- fever*

What to check:
- Is your infant urinating infrequently? (Young children should not go more than eight hours without urinating.) If so, increase liquid consumption.

Treatment:
- Give small amounts of cool liquids frequently if the cause is vomiting (allow a short rest period after the last spell of vomiting). The recommended amount for infants during a six-hour period is six ounces.

*See Fever Guide, pp. 91 to 93

DIAPER RASH

Description: a rash on a baby's bottom in the areas covered by a diaper.

What you need to know:

• Diaper rashes are caused by diapers. The simplest cure is letting your baby go bare-bottomed.

• Yeast is a common cause of persistent diaper rash and requires specific medication for treatment.

• Rubber pants can aggravate the rash.

• Most babies get some form of diaper rash at one time or another.

Supplies: water, baby ointment with zinc oxide.

Get professional help if:

• The rash starts looking angry or the rash pimples develop white heads or blisters.

• Home treatment fails to improve the rash in a few days.

Symptoms:

• red patches, with tiny pimples, on skin areas covered by the diaper

What to check:

• Is the baby allergic to some substance that comes in contact with the red area? Possibilities include rubber pants, disposable diapers, detergents, powders, lanolin, perfumes, alcohol, lotions, and fabric softeners.

Treatment:

• Increase the frequency of diaper changes, cleaning your baby carefully each time with plain water. Let all the water dry before putting on a new diaper.

• Apply zinc oxide ointment between skin and diaper.

• Let the baby go diaperless as much as possible.

DIARRHEA

Description: frequent liquid or soft bowel movements that are light brown or green in color.

What you need to know:

- Causes include viruses, bacteria, parasites, diet change, antibiotics, intolerance to milk.
- Often it is present with colds, sore throat, or infections of the stomach and intestines.
- Diarrhea *alone* rarely leads to dehydration.

Get professional help if:

- Loose bowel movements occur more than once an hour for more than 12 hours.
- There is fever of 102.5°F. (39.1°C.) or higher for more than four hours.*
- Blood is present in stools.

Supplies: thermometer, commercial electrolyte mixes (such as Lytren, Pedialyte), petroleum jelly.

Symptoms:

- liquid or soft bowel movements
- bowel movements increase in frequency to more than two a day

What to check:

- Are there signs of dehydration? (See p. 109.)
- Is your infant passing urine normally?
- How frequent are your infant's bowel movements and what is their consistency?
- Has your infant's diet changed recently?
- Check temperature if he feels warm.

Treatment:

- If the diarrhea is mild (fewer than six to eight watery stools a day), you can usually keep your infant on his normal diet.
- For more severe diarrhea, rest the intestinal tract by stopping breast milk or formula and solid foods for 24 hours.
- During this time, provide clear liquids, in frequent, small amounts, to satisfy thirst and prevent dehydration (they will not cure diarrhea). There is no need to push clear liquids; you merely need to make them available. After 24 hours off food, if your infant is eating solids, begin feeding him fruit, crackers, toast, or cereal.
- On the third day, return to the normal diet.
- Put petroleum jelly or zinc oxide on the buttocks or around the diaper area if it is sore.

*See Fever Guide, pp. 91 to 93

EAR INFECTION

Description: an inflammation or accumulation of fluid in the middle ear, usually caused by bacterial infection.

What you need to know:

- Earaches are common in children under age six.
- Colds often cause the eustachian tubes to swell and close. Fluids build up in the middle ear, causing pain and temporary hearing loss.

Get professional help if:

- Your infant tugs or rubs her ear(s).
- Dizziness or apparent loss of hearing develops.
- Temperature is over 102°F. (38.9°C.).
- Eardrum ruptures. Look for yellow to brown fluid draining from ear.

Supplies: thermometer, acetaminophen, prescribed eardrops, heating pad or hot water bottle.

Symptoms:

- chills/fever*
- congestion, runny nose
- dizziness/headache
- ear discharge
- fussiness/irritability
- inability to sleep
- apparent hearing loss
- rubbing/tugging at ear

What to check:

- Monitor fever.

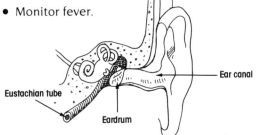

Eustachian tube

Eardrum

Ear canal

Treatment:

- Give acetaminophen, after consulting with your physician.
- You may want to use eardrops (prescribed) to treat pain. Warm the bottle (in hand only); lay infant on back with her head turned to side; pull out, down and back on earlobe. Trickle eardrops into earhole so that they can run all the way in.
- Apply a heating pad or hot water bottle to the ear.
- See a physician, even if treatment relieves the pain.

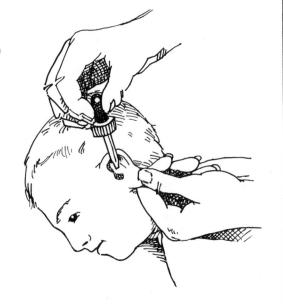

*See Fever Guide, pp. 91 to 93

ECZEMA

Description: an inherited condition characterized by a dry, scaly skin rash and intense itching.

What you need to know:

- The cause is unknown. Outbreaks may be triggered by emotional upset, allergic reaction, or dry winter heat.
- Children with eczema are at increased risk to develop hay fever, asthma, and allergies later in life.
- Eczema often disappears with use of the proper lotions.

Get professional help if:

- Home treatment does not improve the condition within a week.
- The rash becomes infected.

Supplies: OTC or prescribed hydrocortisone ointment, superfatted soap (Basis, Lowila, Aveeno, Oilatum), vaporizer, nail clipper.

Symptoms:

- pink or red rash
- intense itching
- when scratched, rash oozes a moist substance that dries and aggravates itching

What to check:

- Was a new food, clothing, or substance recently introduced to or put on your infant?
- Is soap rinsed thoroughly from your baby's body after baths?
- Do other relatives have eczema?

Treatment:

- Relieve itching with hydrocortisone ointment.
- Use superfatted soap and give baths infrequently.
- Cut your infant's fingernails short (see p. 29) to reduce irritation from scratching. Keep air moist with a vaporizer.

- If a particular food is the cause, eliminate it from your infant's diet. However, do *not* attempt extensive dietary changes without a doctor's supervision.

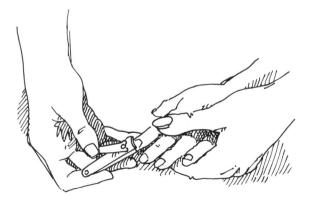

FIFTH DISEASE

Description: a harmless but contagious rash that disappears on its own.

What you need to know:

- The rash usually appears first on the face, looking as if the baby's cheeks have been slapped. A lacy rash may also appear on the trunk.
- It is common, harmless, and self-curing.

Supplies: thermometer.

Get professional help if:

- Your baby has a rash and you believe it is caused by something more serious.

Symptoms:

- red, lacy rash that begins on the face and spreads to back of arms and legs
- fading and intensifying of rash from hour to hour for about ten days

What to check:

- Is there a fever* or any other symptom? If so, the rash is probably not fifth disease.

Treatment:

- There is no treatment and no need for treatment.
- It may recur for weeks, especially in response to skin irritation and temperature extremes. Still, no treatment is required.

*See Fever Guide, pp. 91 to 93

HEARING LOSS

Description: partial or total loss of hearing resulting from a congenital defect, illness, or injury.

What you need to know:

- Sudden loss of hearing is usually temporary and probably indicates blockage of the eardrum by a foreign object, infection or wax.
- A history of deafness in your family should increase your suspicions of hearing loss in your child.

Get professional help if:

- A three-month-old baby does not respond to sound.
- A child does not begin to use a few words by age one.
- At any time you have reason to suspect that your child is not hearing well.

Supplies: thermometer, prescribed medication.

Symptoms:

- lack of response to sounds
- slow speech development
- dizziness
- difficulty with balance, coordination

What to check:

- Have you observed the startle reflex in your newborn? (See p. 12.)
- Try a squeak toy at a quiet time to see if your infant reacts to the sound.

Treatment:

- All conditions that cause an ear infection or hearing loss should be treated by a doctor.
- Do not attempt to remove a foreign object from the ear; see a doctor.
- Do not insert any object—even a cotton swab—into the ear to remove wax. Let your doctor remove the wax at your child's next checkup.

HEAT RASH (PRICKLY HEAT)

Description: small red bumps in skin folds, especially likely to occur on the neck and upper chest of a newborn.

What you need to know:

• Heat rash is very common and causes only minor discomfort.

• The problem is caused by the blockage of pores leading to sweat glands.

Supplies: cool baths.

Get professional help if:

• Blisters appear on the bumps.

Symptoms:

• many tiny red bumps in folds of skin

• most often seen on cheeks, neck, shoulders, creases in skin, and diaper area

What to check:

• Is laundry thoroughly rinsed? Some detergents and bleaches aggravate heat rash.

• Is the baby overdressed? It may contribute to heat rash.

• Are oily skin products blocking pores?

Treatment:

• Keep baby's skin as cool and dry as possible.

• Give frequent, cool baths to help open skin pores.

• Dress the infant as lightly as possible in natural fibers. Put the infant in an air-conditioned environment if possible.

IMPETIGO

Description: a contagious bacterial infection of the skin.

What you need to know:

- Impetigo is contagious, spreading rapidly from one part of the body to another or from child to child through contact.
- Though not serious, it must be treated with care and persistence.

Get professional help if:

- Impetigo seems to be spreading or not responding to home treatment after five days.
- Your infant's urine turns red or cola-colored (a symptom of a rare kidney complication of impetigo).

Supplies: soap and water, compress, OTC antibiotic ointment, nail clipper.

Symptoms:

- yellowish bumps or scabs on the surface of the skin, often occurring in groups, with or without a honey-colored oozing fluid

What to check:

- Since impetigo is contagious, check other family members for signs of infection.
- Make sure each family member uses his or her own towel and washcloth.

Treatment

- Clean the skin with soap and water, then soak sores with a compress for ten minutes.
- Rub away the crust and pus when the crust softens.
- Cover sores with antibiotic cream three times a day. Continue treatment three to four times a day until all sores lose their scabs.

- Clip your infant's nails (see p. 29) to discourage scratching, which spreads the disease.

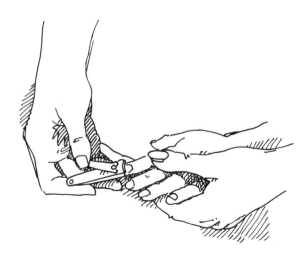

MENINGITIS

Description: a bacterial or viral infection of the membranes surrounding the brain and spinal cord.

What you need to know:
- Meningitis is a serious disease that should be diagnosed and treated by a physician *as soon as possible*.

Supplies: thermometer.

Get professional help if:
- Meningitis symptoms are noted. No single symptom is indicative; look for the combination of symptoms listed.
- If you are unsure or concerned, call your doctor.

Symptoms:
- moderate to high fever*
- vomiting
- prostration, lethargy
- stiff neck (sometimes not in infants)
- purple spots on body (sometimes)

What to check:
- Do you know if your infant has been exposed to meningitis, in a day care setting, for instance? (Not all cases of meningitis are spread person-to-person, however.)

Treatment:
- Meningitis is a serious disease. It should always be treated by a physician. See your doctor *immediately* if you suspect meningitis.

*See Fever Guide, pp. 91 to 93

PINKEYE

Description: an irritation of the linings of the eyelids and the coverings of the whites of the eyes.

What you need to know:

- Many problems cause red eyes and discharge; pinkeye is only one of them.
- It is very contagious.
- Pinkeye is sometimes called conjunctivitis or a cold in the eye.

Supplies: prescribed antibiotics, paper towels.

Get professional help if:

- Your infant has irritated or swollen eyes and you are not sure of the cause. Typical causes: allergies, colds, chlorinated swimming pool water, dust, blocked tear ducts.
- Your infant has recurrent eye irritations.

Symptoms:

- red eyes
- discharge from the eyes after sleep
- swelling of eyelids

What to check:

- Has your infant had contact with someone with pinkeye?

Treatment:

- Home treatment should always be directed by your doctor. Different causes of pinkeye call for different therapies.
- Wash your infant's hands frequently, and wash your hands after touching an infant with pinkeye.
- To protect other family members, use paper towels on the sick infant or isolate his washcloth and towel.
- Discourage eye rubbing.

PNEUMONIA

Description: an infection of the lungs.

What you need to know:
- Pneumonia has several different causes and can occur with greatly varying severity.
- Some forms of pneumonia are contagious; others are not.
- Common colds are *rarely* complicated by pneumonia.

Get professional help if:
- You suspect pneumonia. Your doctor will diagnose the cause of the infection and may prescribe treatment. Very young children may need to be hospitalized.

Supplies: thermometer, prescribed antibiotics (for some pneumonias), acetaminophen.

Symptoms:
- cough
- fever*
- apparent stomach or chest pain
- fast or difficult breathing; infants may flare nostrils and breathe noisily

What to check:
- Does your child seem to be working at breathing?

Treatment:
- If pneumonia is diagnosed, your doctor will treat it.
- Give expectorant cough medicines only if your doctor recommends them.
- Give acetaminophen for fever.

*See Fever Guide, pp. 91 to 93

POISONING

Description: ingestion of medicine, cleaning products, petroleum-based products or other harmful substances.

What you need to know:

• Medicines, cleaners, house plants, and other common items are the chief causes of poisoning. (See pp. 66-67.)

• Safe storage can prevent poisoning, but be ready for emergencies with your local poison-control center phone number.

Supplies: syrup of ipecac, water, milk.

Get professional help if:

• You suspect your infant has swallowed or put into his mouth any harmful substance.

Symptoms:

• abdominal pain/diarrhea
• black-out/unconsciousness
• convulsions
• choking or trouble breathing
• confusion/drowsiness
• coughing up blood/nausea
• dizziness/behavior change
• rash/burn

What to check:

• Have any medicines, cleaners, or other harmful substances been opened, or are any missing?

• Take container and sample of any vomit to hospital.

Treatment:

• Call the poison control center immediately.

• Do not induce vomiting unless you are told to do so. The poison control center will give you instructions on how to use syrup of ipecac (the usual dose is 1 tablespoon, followed by a glass of water).

ROSEOLA

Description: a viral rash affecting young children and infants.

What you need to know:

- Roseola is a common disease in infants of six to twelve months of age.
- There is no prevention or cure, but it goes away on its own.
- The roseola rash *follows* about four days of high fever.
- Your infant is well when the rash disappears, a day or two after it appears.

Get professional help if:

- Your child seems severely affected.
- Symptoms of roseola are accompanied by coughing, vomiting, or diarrhea.
- Fever lasts longer than four days.

Supplies: thermometer, acetaminophen, lukewarm water baths.

Symptoms:

- a high fever of 103 to 105°F. (39.4 to 40.5°C.)*
- rash, developing right after fever drops, with flat, distinct, red spots

What to check:

- Any high fever requires close observation. Diagnosis can only be confirmed when rash appears. By then, if it is *not* roseola, complications could have occurred.

Treatment:

- Treat the fever with acetaminophen and lukewarm water baths as required.
- Watch your infant closely for other symptoms.
- Permit moderate activity if your child feels like it; it does no harm.

*See Fever Guide, pp. 91 to 93

SUDDEN INFANT DEATH SYNDROME (CRIB DEATH)

Description: the sudden death of an apparently normal, healthy infant for reasons that are unknown.

What you need to know:

• Death usually occurs during sleep, within seconds, and without pain.

• Crib death is the leading cause of infant death after the first week of life; each year it strikes 10,000 babies. There is no guaranteed way to prevent crib death.

• It is most common in infants between the ages of one to six months, and rarely occurs after seven months.

• It occurs more often in winter than other seasons, and it occurs worldwide.

• Its cause is not known. Over the years, many explanations have been advanced, but none have been proven, and many have been disproven. It is *not* caused by choking, smothering, strangulation, enlargement of the thymus gland, pneumonia, injury of the spinal cord, or allergy to cow's milk. Current thought is that it may be related to viral infection.

• It's also thought that a baby may be at risk if he was born premature, if he is a twin, or if one of his relatives has died of SIDS. In these cases a physician can decide if the risks warrant putting the baby on a monitor.

• Some infants have slight colds when they die, but there is no evidence that death is related to the cold.

• Since there are no symptoms and the cause is unknown, it is impossible to predict or prevent SIDS. There is no indication that help is needed and no treatment that can be applied.

• Parents and siblings of infants who have died from crib death often feel severe guilt and depression. It is important for them to know the death was *not* due to neglect and is no one's fault—it could not have been prevented. Counseling and contact with other parents may be comforting and helpful; it can be obtained through:

National SIDS Foundation
Two Metro Plaza
8240 Professional Place, Suite 205
Landover, MD 20785
(301) 459-3388

The National SIDS Foundation will refer you to the chapter nearest you, or to other organizations that may be of help.

TEETHING

Description: tenderness of the gums of infants, caused by the eruption of teeth.

What you need to know:

• Not all babies teethe at the same time. It depends on when their teeth erupt. (See pp. 89-90.) Between three months and three years of age is typical.

• Never let a child go to sleep with a bottle of milk or juice. Doing so increases the risk of tooth decay.

Get professional help if:

• Symptoms below are accompanied by signs of illness (fever,* loss of appetite). Teething should not cause a fever; if your baby has a fever, other causes should be considered. Otherwise, professional help is not needed for the eruption of teeth.

Supplies: thermometer, acetaminophen, teething rings, teething biscuits, ice wrapped in a cloth.

Symptoms:

• fussiness

• drooling

• chewing fingers or other objects

• crying

What to check:

• Consider other causes of symptoms: hunger, thirst, boredom, ear infection, a need for affection.

Treatment:

• Little can be done to help teething babies. Cuddling works as well as anything.

• You can try giving acetaminophen to relieve gum soreness.

• Try offering some children teething rings or biscuits, which may help. Some teething babies like to chew cool objects (ice wrapped in cloth or a frozen teething ring). Avoid giving medications sold to relieve teething pain; they have not been proven to work.

*See Fever Guide, pp. 91 to 93

THRUSH

Description: a yeast infection of the mouths and tongues of young children.

What you need to know:

• Thrush causes no symptoms except white patches on the mouth and tongue. It may go away if ignored, but most parents want to treat it.

Supplies: prescribed medication.

Get professional help if:

• Your infant has thrush or you suspect he does.

Symptoms:

• white patches on insides of cheeks, behind lips, or on tongue
• patches look like dried milk, but will not wipe off with a clean handkerchief

What to check:

• Are there blisters inside the infant's mouth? If so, it might be something other than thrush.

Treatment:

• Apply prescribed medication to patches as directed.

URINARY TRACT INFECTION

Description: an infection of the urinary system that can lead to a variety of problems.

What you need to know:

- Urinary tract infections can be tricky to detect and treat, especially in infancy.
- Both boys and girls can be affected by urinary tract infections during the newborn period.
- A physician will often look for a urinary tract infection if she can't find another cause of persistent high fevers.

Get professional help if:

- You detect any sign of urinary tract infection or blockage. Careful diagnosis and subsequent management is called for.

Supplies: thermometer; acetaminophen; juices, especially cranberry juice.

Symptoms:

- frequent, painful, or bloody urination
- discharge
- foul-smelling urine
- apparent abdominal or back pain
- fever*
- nausea

What to check:

- If your infant has a fever over 101°F. (38.3°C.) or appears very ill, call your doctor immediately.

Treatment:

- Treatment must be managed by a physician.
- Until you see your doctor, give acetaminophen for pain and administer large amounts of fluids. Cranberry juice has some antibacterial properties.

*See Fever Guide, pp. 91 to 93

VOMITING

Description: expelling food from stomach through nose and mouth, a common symptom with many causes.

What you need to know:

- The most common cause of vomiting, by far, is a stomach viral infection.
- Infants often spit up, but this is not vomiting.
- The main concern with vomiting is dehydration.

Get professional help if:

- Any vomiting does not stop within 12 hours or is combined with drowsiness, apparent abdominal pain, high fever,* labored breathing.
- Vomited material is yellow or green more than once or twice.
- Your infant vomits *forcefully* shortly after being fed.

Supplies: thermometer; commercial electrolyte mixes (such as Lytren, Pedialyte); light foods (Jello, broth, apple juice)

What to check:

- Look for signs of dehydration: listlessness, dry mouth, sunken eyes, crying without tears, infrequent urination.

Treatment:

- Watch infants under five months closely and call your doctor if vomiting persists.
- Wait a while after your infant vomits. Then offer cool liquids in frequent small amounts (one teaspoon to one tablespoon at ten-minute intervals).
- Increase clear liquids gradually. Do *not* feed chicken broth, which contains fat and may be difficult to digest.
- Keep the child on clear liquids for a day. If your child is on solid food, allow light foods first (Jello, applesauce, dry toast, rice, bananas), then a regular diet.

*See Fever Guide, pp. 91 to 93

APPENDIX

GUIDE TO RESOURCES

BOOKS

CHILD DEVELOPMENT

Brazelton, T. Berry. *Infants and Mothers* (Delacorte).
Caplan, Frank. *The First 12 Months of Life* (Bantam).
Hagstrom, Julie and Joan Morrill. *Games Babies Play* (A & W Visual Library).
Levy, Dr. Janine. *The Baby Exercise Book* (Pantheon).

PARENTING

Kelly, Marguerite and Elia S. Parsons. *Mother's Almanac* (Doubleday).
Lansky, Vicki. *Dear Babysitter* (Meadowbrook).
--------. *Practical Parenting Tips* (Meadowbrook).
Sullivan, S. Adams. *Father's Almanac* (Doubleday).

FOOD AND NUTRITION

Eiger, M.D., Marvin S. and Sally Wendklos Olds. *The Complete Book of Breastfeeding* (Bantam).
La Leche League. *The Womanly Art of Breastfeeding* (La Leche League).
Lansky, Vicki. *Feed Me! I'm Yours* (Meadowbrook).

MEDICAL CARE

Hart, M.D., Terril H. *The Parents' Guide to Baby and Child Medical Care* (Meadowbrook).
Pantell, M.D., Robert H. et al. *Taking Care of Your Child* (Addison Wesley).

MAGAZINES AND NEWSLETTERS

American Baby, 575 Lexington Ave., New York, NY 10022, (212) 752-0775. Monthly; for expecting parents through those of one-year-olds.
Baby Talk, 185 Madison Ave., New York, NY 10016, (212) 679-4400. Monthly; for expecting parents through those of two-year-olds.
Growing Child, 22 N. Second St., Lafayette, IN 47902, (317) 423-2624. Monthly; for parents of newborns through those of six-year-olds.
Mothers Today, 441 Lexington Ave., New York, NY 10017, (212) 867-4820. Bimonthly; for expecting parents through parents of four-year-olds.
Mothering, Box 2208, Albuquerque, NM 87103, (505) 867-3110. Quarterly; for parents of newborns through those of five-year olds, though some articles cover older children.
Parents Magazine, 685 Third Ave., New York, NY 10017, (212) 878-8700. Monthly; for expecting parents through those of pre-teenagers.
Pediatrics for Parents, 176 Mount Hope Ave., Bangor, ME 04401, (207) 942-6212. Monthly; for expecting parents through those of teenagers.
Practical Parenting Newsletter, 18326A Minnetonka Blvd., Deephaven, MN 55391, (612) 475-1505. Bimonthly; for expecting parents through those of grade-schoolers.
Working Mother, 230 Park Ave., New York, NY 10169, (212) 551-9412. Monthly; for parents of infants through pre-schoolers.

RESOURCE GROUPS

American Academy of Pediatrics, Office of Public Education, 1801 Hinman Ave., Evanston, IL 60204; (312) 869-4255. Free list of publications on such topics as car seats, infectious diseases, accidents, child abuse, day care, drugs, nutrition, handicaps, genetic screening.

American Red Cross. Contact your local chapter to get information on the many courses and pamphlets available. Not all programs are available through all chapters. Some of the courses offered include first aid, family health and home nursing, swimming, parenting and C.P.R. (cardiopulmonary resuscitation).

Department of Health and Welfare, Poison Control Product Information Section, Laboratory Center for Disease Control, LCDC Building, Tunney's Pasture, Ottawa, Ontario K1A OL2, Canada; (613) 992-0979.

International Childbirth Education Association, P.O. Box 20048, Minneapolis, MN 55420; (612) 854-8660. Local services include childbirth education classes; health-care referrals on request. Free publications list.

La Leche League International, 9616 Minneapolis Avenue, Franklin Park, IL 60131, (312) 455-7730. Self-help organization for mothers, encouraging breast-feeding. Local weekly meetings; trained counselors can also answer questions by phone. Free publications list available upon request.

National Committee for the Prevention of Child Abuse, P.O. Box 2866, Chicago, IL 60690; (312) 663-3520. Provides informational packets on child abuse.

National Genetics Foundation, Inc., 555 West 57th Street, NY 10019; (212) 586-5800. Directs people in need of genetic services to them. Provides and reviews questionnaires on family health history. Free publications list.

National Institute of Mental Health, 5600 Fishers Lane, Parklawn Building, Room 15C17, Rockville, MD 20857; (301) 443-4515. Answers requests for mental health information for the public. Pamphlets and single free copies of publications on children's mental health, autism, and depression are available.

National Poison Center Network, 125 Desoto Street, Pittsburgh, PA 15213; (412) 647-5600. Offers home poison control materials. Sheet of 12 Mr. Yuk stickers, $1. Home poison prevention education kit and poison plant list, a list of 50 possibly toxic indoor and outdoor plants, available for nominal fees.

Parents Anonymous (P.A.) Hotline: in California, (800) 352-0386; outside California, (800) 421-0353. Offers on-the-spot counseling and a price list of nine items (booklets, pamphlets, etc.) parents can get to help prevent child abuse.

Parents Campaign for Handicapped Children and Youth, 1201 16th Street NW, Washington, D.C. 20036; (202) 822-7900. Booklet available for $2.00.

Parents Without Partners, Inc., 7910 Woodmont Avenue, Bethesda, MD 20814; (301) 654-8850. Provides support through family educational and adult activity programs conducted by local volunteers. Information on seminars, community workshops, support groups, and publications for single parents available upon request.

Physicians for Automotive Safety, P.O. Box 208, Rye, NY 10580; (914) 253-9525. Publishes a pamphlet, available for 50¢, that describes recommended car seats and other safety restraints for infants and children. Includes names and descriptions of crash-tested infant carriers and infant/toddler seats currently on the market.

U.S. Consumer Product Safety Commission, Washington, DC 20207; (800) 638-2772. Provides information on the safety and effectiveness of various products.

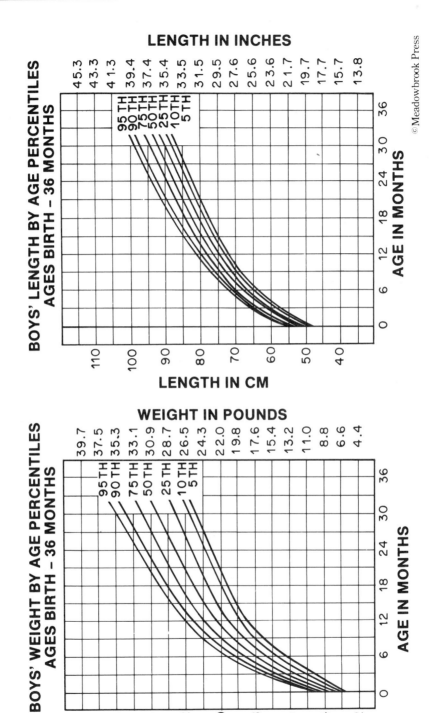

LENGTH IN INCHES

BOYS' LENGTH BY AGE PERCENTILES AGES BIRTH – 36 MONTHS

95TH 90TH 75TH 50TH 25TH 10TH 5TH

AGE IN MONTHS

LENGTH IN CM

©Meadowbrook Press

WEIGHT IN POUNDS

BOYS' WEIGHT BY AGE PERCENTILES AGES BIRTH – 36 MONTHS

95TH 90TH 75TH 50TH 25TH 10TH 5TH

AGE IN MONTHS

WEIGHT IN KG

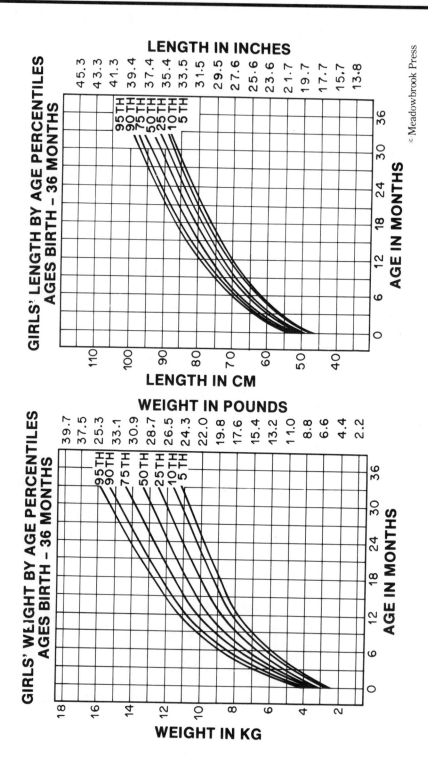

LENGTH IN INCHES

GIRLS' LENGTH BY AGE PERCENTILES
AGES BIRTH – 36 MONTHS

45.3 43.3 41.3 39.4 37.4 35.4 33.5 31.5 29.5 27.6 25.6 23.6 21.7 19.7 17.7 15.7 13.8

95TH 90TH 75TH 50TH 25TH 10TH 5TH

AGE IN MONTHS

LENGTH IN CM

110 100 90 80 70 60 50 40

WEIGHT IN POUNDS

GIRLS' WEIGHT BY AGE PERCENTILES
AGES BIRTH – 36 MONTHS

39.7 37.5 25.3 33.1 30.9 28.7 26.5 24.3 22.0 19.8 17.6 15.4 13.2 11.0 8.8 6.6 4.4 2.2

95TH 90TH 75TH 50TH 25TH 10TH 5TH

AGE IN MONTHS

WEIGHT IN KG

18 16 14 12 10 8 6 4 2

INDEX

See the Symptoms Index (p. 94) for symptoms associated with specific illnesses and injuries.

A

Accident prevention
  See Safety.
Acetaminophen doses, 92
Acne (newborn), 95
Allergies, food, 59
Apgar tests, 9

B

Baby care and handling, 15-39
  Holding, 16
  Picking up, 16-17
  Swaddling, 16-17
Baby exercises, 85
Baby food, preparing, 61-62
Babysitters, 72
Backpack, 69
Bathing, 24-29
  Sponge baths, 24-25
  Tub baths, 26-28
Birthmarks, 8
Biting, 46
  See also Teething.
Books, 83
  See also Toys.
Bottlefeeding, 2, 42, 51-56
Bowel movements, 18, 19, 90
  See also Constipation, Diarrhea.
Breastfeeding, 2, 42-50
Breathing emergency, 96
Bronchiolitis, 97
Burns, 91
Burping, 57

C

Car seat, 68
  See also Furniture and equipment.
Cardiac arrest, 98
Checkups, medical 88-89
  Schedule, 88
  See also Immunizations, Medical care.
Child-proofing, 64-67
  See also Safety.
Choking, 13, 99
Circumcision
  Care, 29
  Making decision about, 2

Clothing, 35-39
  Newborn, 37-38
  Older baby, 38
  Outdoor, 39
  Shoes and socks, 36
Cold, 100
Colic, 33, 101
Colostrum, 44
  See also Breastfeeding.
Concussion, 102
Constipation, 18, 103
Convulsion, 90, 104
Cough, 105
Cradle cap
  See Seborrhea.
Crib, 30, 68-69
  See also Furniture and equipment.
Crib death
  See Sudden infant death syndrome.
Crossed eyes, 11, 107
Croup, 108
Crying, causes of and comforts for, 33

D

Dehydration, 109, 111
Dental care, 55, 89-90
  See also Teeth, Teething.
Development, baby, 73-80
  First month, 74
  Second month, 74-75
  Third month, 75-76
  Fourth month, 76
  Fifth month, 76
  Sixth month, 77
  Seventh month, 77-78
  Eighth month, 78
  Ninth month, 78-79
  Tenth month, 79
  Eleventh month, 80
  Twelfth month, 80
Diaper rash, 110
  See also Rashes.
Diapers, 19-23
  Care, 21
  Folding, 23
  How to diaper, 22-23
Diarrhea, 18, 90, 111

Special Gift Books

The Best Baby Name Book In The Whole Wide World

America's best-selliong baby name book by Burce and Vicki Lansky. More names, more up-to-date, more helpful, more entertaining, more gifty than any other baby name book! — *over 10,000 boys' and girls' names . . . more than any other book — how to name your baby: 15 rules — name psychology and stereotypes.* **Only $3.75 ppd.**

Free Stuff For Kids

Over 250 of the best free and up-to-a-dollar things kids can get by mail: — *badges & buttons — games, kits & puzzles — coins, bills & stamps — bumper stickers & decals — coloring & comic books — posters & maps — seeds & rocks.* FREE STUFF FOR KIDS is America's No. 1 best-selling book for children! **Only $3.75 ppd.**

Hi Mom! Hi Dad!

101 cartoons about all the funny things that happen after you get your baby home, during the first twelve months of parenthood. It's a great remedy for post-partum blues.

$4.30 ppd.

Do They Ever Grow Up?

A hilarious, 101-cartoon survival guide for parents of the tantrum and pacifer set. It's all about the terrible two's and the pre-school years. Lynn Johnston's funniest book yet!

$4.30 ppd.

David, We're Pregnant

101 laughing-out-loud cartoons by Lynn Johnston that accentuate the humorous side of conceiving, expecting and giving birth. It turns all the little worries of pregnancy into laughter.

$4.30 ppd.

My First Years

A beautiful baby record book to save your precious memories from arrival day to kindergarten! The colorful padded cover is reproduced from an original cross-stitch design of the *My First Friends* animals, with a delicate framing border. There are 32 pages of popular subjects like the family tree, a growth record, medical history, the first birthday, favorite photos, and many more. It is also gift boxed to be the perfect shower or new-arrival gift. **$13.75**

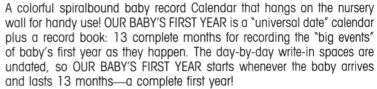

Our Baby's First Year

A colorful spiralbound baby record Calendar that hangs on the nursery wall for handy use! OUR BABY'S FIRST YEAR is a "universal date" calendar plus a record book: 13 complete months for recording the "big events" of baby's first year as they happen. The day-by-day write-in spaces are undated, so OUR BABY'S FIRST YEAR starts whenever the baby arrives and lasts 13 months—a complete first year!

Each month features a colorful baby animal nursery character to decorate the room, plus month-by-month development and baby care tips for quick reference. There's even a family tree and birth record form! A colorful and practical baby gift! **$9.50 ppd.**

Parents' Guide To Baby & Child Medical Care

A first aid and home treatment guide that shows parents how to handle over 150 common childhood illnesses in step-by-step illustrated treatment format. Edited by Terril H. Hart, M.D., it contains: — *index of symptoms — record forms — height and weight charts — accident prevention — childproofing tips.* **Only $8.75 ppd.**

"If you have a new baby, you need this book. It is really the most useful baby medical guide available."
—Mitch Einzig, M.D.
Children's Health Center,
Minneapolis, MN

Vicki Lansky Books

Feed Me! I'm Yours
by Vicki Lansky

America's most popular baby food and tot cookbook. Over 200 recipes and ideas for easy and economical ways to make baby food and for sneaking nutrition into infants, toddlers and tots. Practical, gifty, spiral-bound edition — *Corn off the Cob Hot Cereal — M&M Cookies — Egg Posies — Simpler Souffle — Valentine Crispies — Bunny Biscuits — plus milk-free cooking, travel food recipes, kitchen crafts and more.* **Only $6.75 ppd.**

The Taming Of The C.A.N.D.Y.Monster
by Vicki Lansky

The No. 1 N.Y. Times bestseller for getting kids to eat less sugary, salty junk food. Over 200 recipes for more nutritious snakcs, desserts, brown-bag lunches, plus shopping tips, humorous glossary and more — *Good 'n Easy Frosting — Little Bit-of-Chocolate Bars — Unbirthday Cake — Banana Smoothie Drink — Lazybones Applesauce — Better-For-You Brownies and more.* **Only $6.75 ppd.**

Practical Parenting Tips
by Vicki Lansky

Over 1,000 parent-tested ideas for baby and child care that you won't find in Dr. Spock's books. Vicki's newest bestseller is the most helpful collection of new, down-to-earth ideas from new parents ever published. Practical ideas for saving time, trouble and money on such topics as: — *new baby care — car travel — toilet training — dressing kids for less — discipline — self-esteem.* **Only $6.75 ppd.**

Dear Babysitter
by Vicki Lansky

Peace of mind at least! For new parents who finally get to go out to a movie again, here's a way to make sure the kids *and* the sitter are safe and happy. Really *two* ways: DEAR BABYSITTER includes a 48-page Sitter's Handbook of basic first aid and emergency procedures, games and activity suggestions for all age levels up to 7, techniques for enforcing your "house rules", and bedtime strategies.

This permanent babysitter's "kit" includes a refillable Instruction Pad for recording contact numbers and other special information for each sitter, each night. What a gift for new (or veteran) moms—and for sitters too! **$9.00 ppd.**

Name _____

Address _____

City _____ State _____ Zip _____

Please charge my ☐ Visa ☐ Mastercharge Account

Accnt. # _____ Exp. Date _____

Signature _____

Check or money order payable to Meadowbrook Press.

Quant.	Title	Cost Per Book	AMOUNT

We do not ship C.O.D. Postage and handling included in all prices. **Total**

Your group or organization may qualify for group quantity discounts: please write for further information to Marjie Cargill, Meadowbrook Press. 18318 Minnetonka Blvd., Deephaven, MN 55391

Meadowbrook Press
18318 Minnetonka Boulevard • Deephaven, Minnesota 55391